THE COMPLETE HANDGUN
1300 TO THE PRESENT

A US Navy officer cleans his Colt M1911A1 during the Second World War

THE COMPLETE
HANDGUN
1300 TO THE PRESENT

Ian V Hogg and John Batchelor

Exeter Books

NEW YORK

in association with Phoebus

Copyright © 1979
Phoebus Publishing Company/
BPC Publishing Limited
52 Poland Street, London W1A 2JX

First published in USA 1979 by
Exeter Books
Distributed by Bookthrift, Inc.
New York, NY 10018

ISBN 0-89673-024-7
Library of Congress Number
79-5055

This material first appeared in
Handguns 1300–1978 © 1979
Phoebus Publishing Company/
BPC Publishing Limited and

Handguns 1870–1978 © 1978
Phoebus Publishing Company/
BPC Publishing Limited

Made and printed in Great Britain
by Redwood Burn Limited

A Royal Navy rating and an Army officer give pistol instruction to a group of women in the First World War

Introduction

The first handgun evolved from the experiments of men like the Black Monk Berthold who is credited with the discovery of gunpowder in the 14th century. These weapons were crude devices which could be as dangerous to the firer as the enemy. The 'hand-gonnes' were clumsy and inaccurate and gunsmiths were constantly trying to improve their designs. The first innovation was the matchlock which involved a simple trigger with a length of smouldering cord for touching off the gunpowder.

Wheel-locks and later flintlocks did away with the hazards of carrying a burning slow match. The wheel-lock was a complex mechanism which was costly to produce and beyond the pocket of the common soldier. *The Complete Handgun: 1300 to the Present* contains illustrations by John Batchelor of some of these fine examples of the gunmakers' art.

The text, by Ian Hogg, covers the men as well as the weapons, for although the early handguns were made by anonymous craftsmen, the pistols of the late 19th and early 20th century have clearly traceable pedigrees. The pressures of war and the complexities of patent law shaped their designs as much as inventive genius. Handguns often became famous under the names of men who knew little or nothing about weapons but had a flair for publicity and the ability to cash in on new inventions.

By the end of the 19th century, handgun design was moving from the revolver to the self-loading automatic. The revolver still remains popular, however, and although this book includes such fine automatics as the Colt .45 M1911 and the PO8 Luger, it also contains revolvers like the Colt Peacemaker and the Webley .38 Mk4.

Despite their short range and comparative inaccuracy, handguns have changed history as the assassin's weapon and as the mass issue personal arm for tank crews and officers. The world has lost tyrants and heroes to the handgun. Men have prized and praised the pistol and reviled it as a hopeless medium-range man-stopper – this is its story from the 14th century to the present day.

IAN V. HOGG enlisted in the Royal Artillery during the Second World War and served in Europe and the Far East – including Korea – before becoming an Assistant Instructor in Gunnery at the Royal School of Artillery. In 1966 he joined the staff of the Royal Military College of Science, from which he retired in 1972 with the rank of Master Gunner to become a professional writer.

JOHN BATCHELOR, after serving in the RAF, worked in the technical publications departments of several British aircraft firms before becoming a freelance artist. His work has appeared in a wide range of books and magazines, and his work for Purnell's History of the World War Specials has established him as one of the leading artists in his field.

Editors: Christy Campbell
Will Fowler
Art Editor: Roger Hammond
Production: Sheila Biddlecombe

J G Moore

A Royal Naval Air Service Flight Lieutenant takes aim with a Webley and Scott .455 automatic pistol

Contents

'HAND-GONNES'

According to the best available records, the gun appeared around about 1325 AD. Gunpowder had made its appearance some 75 years before, as a pyrotechnic substance, making smoke and flame for amusement or alarm. The origins of gunpowder are shrouded in mystery; it has been attributed to the Chinese, to the Arabs, the Turks and to several others but without much real evidence being offered. Undoubtedly the Chinese were adept at the manufacture of fireworks, but this is by no means the same thing as developing gunpowder. There is certainly no record of the substance before the famous anagram of Friar Bacon which he published in 1242, and yet by 1268, in another publication, Bacon referred to 'The powder, known in diverse places, composed of saltpetre, charcoal and sulphur'. So in just over twenty years gunpowder had passed from being a mystery divulged to the few to being something 'known in diverse places'.

How the powder came to be developed as an agent for propelling projectiles is another mystery. The most famous story, which is still to be found repeated as truth, is the myth of 'Black Berthold' the mysterious monk of Freiburg in Germany, who, one fateful day, took to pounding a mixture of charcoal, sulphur and saltpetre in a mortar. The mixture exploded and blew the pestle from Berthold's hand, and he, after recovering from the shock, put two and two together and sat down to invent the gun. As a byproduct, we are told, the word 'mortar' commemorates this event.

It's a nice story and one which has inspired a number of artists over the years. Unfortunately the 'facts' offered in confirmation do not hold up against any sort of critical examination. The year 1340 is offered as the moment of Black Berthold's revelation by one authority, 1354 by another and 1380 by a third. All of these fall well after the first absolutely authentic mention of cannon, so they cannot be taken seriously. Moreover, more recent research tends to show that

Berthold Schwartz (Black Berthold) in the process of discovering gunpowder during experiments in Freiburg, Germany in the 14th century

Black Berthold himself never existed outside the pages of storybooks.

In 1325 one Walter de Millimete wrote a text for the young Edward III of England, entitled *On the Duties of Kings* and among the illustrations is a picture of a cannon. No explanation is advanced in the text; there is evidence pointing to the fact that the pictures were drawn first and the manuscript written afterwards and that correlation between the two was of no great import in those days. But this is undoubtedly the first representation of a cannon which can be positively dated, and, equally undoubtedly, it predates Black Berthold by a good few years. In the following year, 1326, the records of the city of Florence record the manufacture of brass cannon and iron balls for the defence of the 'commune, camps and territory of Florence', and from then on the history of the gun is moderately well documented.

The gun in its earliest days was probably an inefficient device by our standards, but that was neither here nor there; it worked, and that was sufficient wonder at the time. Whether or not the ball (or arrow) which it discharged actually hit somebody was beside the point; the flash and bang and the cloud of smoke were enough to put the fear of the Devil into the opposition. And for this reason the early guns were cannon, large weapons which had to be lugged into position before the battle, fired, and then left alone because they were unlikely to be reloaded before the tide of battle had washed over them leaving them either high and dry behind their own lines, or captured and within the enemy lines. Another factor contributing to their size was that the whole business still smacked of black magic and nobody was very sure what was happening, or why it happened. And therefore it was as well to confine this mysterious force into something fairly strong and touch it off at arms length.

Just when the gun shrank in size to something capable of being handled by one man is not clear. One theory which has been advanced is that the handgun came about by a gradual diminution of the cannon. The original cannon were, as we have already said, large weapons which had a slow rate of fire. Because of this they were of little value against a mass of troops, since their one or two shots could do little but bowl over one or two of the opposition. In an effort to spread the effect, the 'ribaudequin' was produced; the guns were made smaller and a number of them, splayed out so as to spread their collective fire, were mounted on a light cart; these weapons are mentioned as early as 1382, in use by the burghers of Ghent. But a number of ribaudequin barrels immovably clamped to the bed of a cart, while they had a good effect, were restricted in their distribution; they could all be fired in their set direction, but there was no scope to deal with the odd enemy who appeared off to a flank. The logical step, it would seem, would be to take the barrels off the cart, fit them into some convenient wooden frame that a man could hold, and give one to each soldier so that he could fire it in whatever direction the target appeared. And in this way the handgun arrived. This, at present, seems the most reasonable theory.

The 'hand-gonne' appeared some time in the latter part of the 14th century; there is no doubt of this, since the oldest extant firearm was excavated from an old well in Tannenberg Castle, and it is a matter of record that the castle was overthrown in 1399, so the weapon had obviously rested there

A medieval gunner touches off a seige cannon. These crude pieces were later mounted on carts for easier transport. Gunners were often civilian contractors who brought their pieces to the battlefield and left when they thought they were under threat from a serious enemy attack. Since they had built their own guns this was a pardonable attitude by modern standards, but gunners found that a smaller piece was handy for close defence if they failed to make good their escape. From these crude beginnings evolved the 'hand-gonne' which began life as the weapon of the wealthy innovator

AN EARLY THREE-BARRELLED HANDGUN

This crude weapon was mounted on the end of a pole and gave the soldier of the time a spread of three shots when he touched off the charge. The barrels are linked together with iron hoops

from before that time. The general form was that of a wrought barrel anything from six inches to a yard in length secured by iron bands to a rough wooden stock of three to five feet in length. In many cases these weapons were provided for the defence of castles and towns, to be fired from the walls, and in order to reduce the recoil force on the firer they were fitted with hooks under the muzzle which could be hooked over the wall. This form of construction led to the German term *hakenbuchse* from which, by corruption, the word 'arquebus' was derived. The smaller weapons, though, could be fired by a standing man, provided he took a secure grip of it before loosing it off. The manner of taking this grip, allied with the manner of firing the weapon, pretty well ruined any chance of accuracy, even supposing the weapons to be capable of accurate shooting. The normal stance, as depicted in various early engravings, was to grip the stock behind the barrel with the left hand, and tuck the remainder of the stock beneath the arm, holding it into the side with the elbow. To fire, it was necessary to take a burning stick or brand and present it to the vent of the gun, in which a sprinkling of gunpowder was exposed. This would be lit, would flash down the vent, and thus fire the charge inside the gun chamber to shoot the ball. Obviously, bringing a burning brand into contact with the powder was a task which had to be observed

carefully; if the firer was standing gazing at his enemy, he might well miss the vent and press the burning end on to his own left hand or even miss the gun entirely. So he attended very carefully to what he was doing, manipulating the brand in his right hand. It follows that he wasn't looking at the target and wasn't devoting all his energy to gripping the gun; so it is unreasonable to expect any accuracy, and anyone who was hit was most unlikely to have been the original target.

Sometime early in the 15th century some unrecorded experimenter discovered that soaking a piece of twine in a solution of saltpetre and then allowing it to dry produced a 'slow match' or cord which could be lit and which would slowly burn away, providing its owner with a constant source of ignition. Gunners soon adopted this for the ignition of cannon, looping the match round a special stick called a 'linestock'. Arquebusiers also adopted the match as a form of ignition, carrying a loop in their hand and applying it to the vent of their gun when ready to fire. And it was only a short step from this to the development of a metal arm on the side of the gun, S-shaped, which would hold a piece of burning slow match in its upper part. When pulled away from the gun, it was safe to load and prime. When ready to fire the lower limb of the S was drawn back, so that the upper limb, with the match, went forward and pressed the burning end of the match on to the vent to fire the gun.

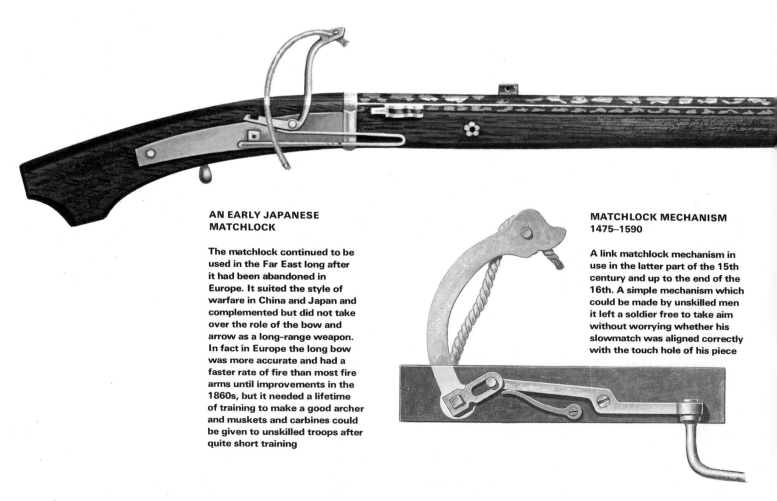

AN EARLY JAPANESE MATCHLOCK

The matchlock continued to be used in the Far East long after it had been abandoned in Europe. It suited the style of warfare in China and Japan and complemented but did not take over the role of the bow and arrow as a long-range weapon. In fact in Europe the long bow was more accurate and had a faster rate of fire than most fire arms until improvements in the 1860s, but it needed a lifetime of training to make a good archer and muskets and carbines could be given to unskilled troops after quite short training

MATCHLOCK MECHANISM 1475–1590

A link matchlock mechanism in use in the latter part of the 15th century and up to the end of the 16th. A simple mechanism which could be made by unskilled men it left a soldier free to take aim without worrying whether his slowmatch was aligned correctly with the touch hole of his piece

A battle-axe and pistol combination which left the 16th-century soldier with a handy weapon after he had discharged his pistol

The first firing mechanism, the 'Match Lock' had been born.

In this original form the matchlock was a little less than perfect, but towards the end of the 15th century it began to show improvement. The simple system of an S-shaped piece of metal was replaced by a slightly more complex arrangement; the match-holder was cut in half, and the lower section discarded, after which a spring was arranged to drive it forward into the vent of the gun. It could now be pulled back by the operator until it was held by a thumb-catch or a finger-operated trigger. The gun was now loaded and the vent primed, after which the firer took aim and released the catch or trigger. The spring thrust the match forward to make contact with the powder, and the gun fired—sometimes. Sometimes it didn't because the match was slammed forward so fast it was extinguished before it could light the powder in the vent, whereupon the gunner had to recock and then get out flint and tinder and relight the match before he could continue.

This arrangement became known as the 'snapping match-lock' and although it was not to last long in Europe before being superseded by better ideas, it persisted for several hundred years in India, Japan and other parts of the East. This was because the matchlock had been introduced into Japan by the Portuguese shortly before the country was closed to foreigners; the matchlock worked, and the Japanese were under no pressure to improve it, so it was still a prominent weapon in the 19th century. Its introduction to India is not easily credited to any particular band of explorers, since several moved into that area in the 15th century, but the simplicity of the matchlock recommended itself to the native workmen, and, again, it continued to be used there long after it had died out elsewhere.

The matchlock had other drawbacks beside the mechanical ones; for one thing, the whole system was dependent upon the gunner keeping his match alight, and if the rain came, then he was out of action. Sentries walking about at night with their lighted match advertised their presence, as did attacking troops at dawn or dusk. There was always the risk of an accident, when a man was walking around with a lighted match in his hand and festooned with packets and flasks of gunpowder, and many a soldier of those days sustained severe burns and wounds without ever seeing an enemy.

It was inevitable that with the advance of mechanical ingenuity in other fields, that the ignition system of the gun would be improved, and that improvement came along early in the 16th century. Its inventor has never been identified, but logic points to it having been developed in southern

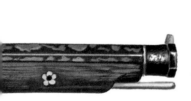

Six of the 36 positions to load and fire a 17th-century matchlock musket. The musketeer carried 12 measured charges of gunpowder slung from his bandolier as well as his musket balls. The sword was for use in close-quarter defence

Ownership of firearms was originally reserved for the wealthy who could afford to have the parts worked and embellished by skilled craftsmen

Fotomas Index

ITALIAN WHEEL-LOCK ABOUT 1640

The wheel-lock system was based on a serrated wheel which unwound under tension rather like a fast clockwork motor. The serrations engaged a chunk of iron pyrites and struck a stream of sparks which ignited the powder in the pan on the side of the pistol firing the piece

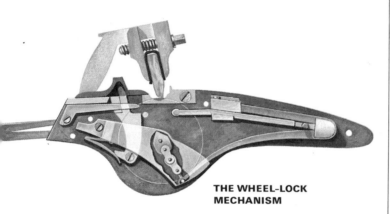

THE WHEEL-LOCK MECHANISM

The advantage of this system was that it saved a soldier from carrying a lighted match to ignite the charge in his handgun. The disadvantage was that it was a costly piece of machinery which was beyond the pocket of most ordinary soldiers or the exchequer

COMBINED WHEEL-LOCK KEY AND SPANNER

The combination tool for stripping modern rifles is no innovation and this tool was used for winding up the spring in a wheel-lock gun. The wheel-lock might be reliable and safe, but it took time to be made ready for action and could not be recharged in the heat of battle

Germany or Switzerland, since much of the mechanical aspect of the new invention seems to have derived from clockmaking techniques. This was the wheel-lock.

The wheel-lock takes its name from the principal feature of the mechanism – a serrated wheel which, when rapidly revolved, strikes sparks from a piece of iron pyrites held against it by spring pressure. By careful design, the stream of sparks was directed into the vent of the gun, now enlarged to form a 'pan' of generous dimensions which held a charge of powder sufficient to ensure rapid ignition. The axle upon which the wheel revolved was connected to a length of chain, and the other end of this chain was attached to a mainspring. The end of the axle was shaped into a square which could be gripped by a crank or key. To prepare the weapon, the firer put the key onto the squared end of the axle and wound it, thus pulling on the chain and loading the spring. When sufficient tension had been applied he removed the key, and the wheel remained stationary because it was locked by a sear or strip of metal which dropped into one of the serrations on the outer surface of the wheel. The lid of the pan was now slipped forward and the pan primed with powder. Pulling the lid back to protect the powder brought the pyrites into contact with the wheel and it was retained there by a spring. When the trigger was pulled, the sear came away from the wheel, the spring pulled on the chain, the wheel revolved, and the serrations struck sparks from the pyrites and shot them into the pan.

The virtues of the wheel-lock were many; in the first place there was no longer the variety of hazards connected with carrying around a lighted match. In the second place the weapon could be cocked and carried ready for instant use, and, provided the pan was a tight fit, even rain was unlikely to interfere with its action. Should the firer so wish, he could make the weapon safe by sliding the pan cover and pyrites away from the wheel and then press the trigger; no sparks would result and the weapon was rendered safe. Equally, he could leave it with the wheel cocked but with the pyrites out of contact, so that it was safe but so that a quick movement of the pan cover would bring the weapon to readiness.

But the wheel-lock had one additional virtue which makes it of particular importance to the study of the handgun. because it was now possible to carry a gun without the need to carry a burning match, it became feasible to carry a gun more or less permanently, on the person. and from this it became a short step to carrying a concealed gun, provided that the weapon could be made small enough. And once the opportunity for carrying small guns appeared, the mechanical ingenuity needed to manufacture small guns was not far behind. And in this way the wheel-lock paved the way for the one-hand-gun or pistol.

At this time the firearm was still primarily a military arm, largely because of the expense of owning one and because anyone with enough money to own one and the desire to own one was probably a military man in some way or another, even if only during the war. As a result the first pistols were far from being the tiny pocket weapons common today; they were long, heavy and not particularly graceful devices, made strong enough to be used as a club for use after they had been fired or if the mechanism failed in any way. They became the standard equipment of cavalry, replacing the pikes and lances, swords and axes of earlier periods. The tactic which evolved was a rapid gallop toward the enemy, then the collected discharge of a brace of pistols at short range by every man in the front rank, followed by a wheel to a flank to allow the second rank to fire and wheel away and so on. This was a pretty devastating method of attack against standing troops who were, by this time, well used to using muskets and pikes to repel cavalry but who were somewhat put out by this novel and apparently foolproof procedure. The German cavalry of Charles V perfected this technique and made their name with it, and it took quite a while before a suitable riposte was discovered. Eventually it was realised that instead of sitting there and letting the pistol-wielding cavalry have their own way, the infantry should suddenly break out and charge the horse soldiers, who, so infatuated with their new technique, had probably discarded their swords and lances and forgotten their elementary drills, so that they were sitting ducks for the foot soldiers.

For the bulk of the soldiery however, the matchlock was still the standard weapon, and for one very good reason; the wheel-lock, for all its advantages, was an expensive piece of equipment and one which needed cossetting by its owner. The rough and tumble of the battlefield could soon ruin a delicate wheel-lock; the cocking key was easily lost; the soft iron pyrites soon wore away, and was not in common supply; and if anything about the lock were to break, then it required the services of a skilled artisan, whereas a matchlock could be mended by any handy blacksmith.

If these features militated against the wheel-lock for military use, they were no hindrance to its adoption by hunters and sportsmen once they grasped the advantage to be gained by a ready-to-use weapon, and soon the gunsmiths began to vie with each other to produce weapons which were not only efficient but which were graceful, elegant, and decorated in a manner befitting the station of the nobleman or other monied individual who was going to buy the pistol. It has truly been observed that there is rarely such a thing as an elegant and beautiful matchlock, and there is no such thing as a rough and ugly wheel-lock; only those with money could afford them and they had every intention of obtaining the best for their money.

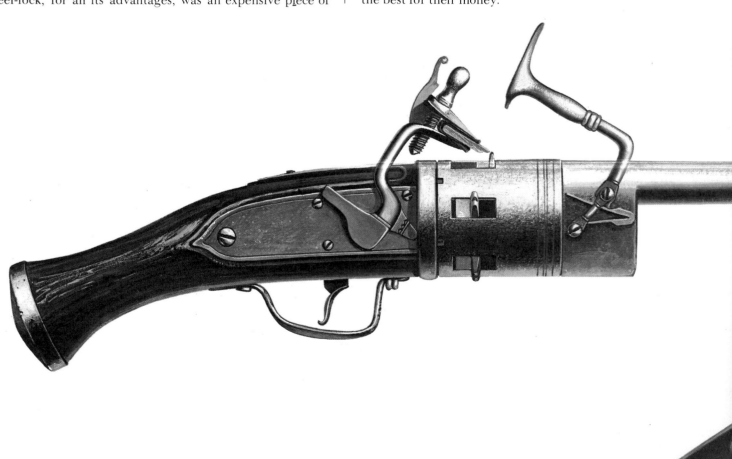

A musketeer loads his weapon using a powder horn to drop a measured amount of gunpowder down the barrel. A smaller powder horn for priming the matchlock hangs from his hip

Fotomas Index

The wheel-lock was not amenable to any great modification, but over the years skilled gunsmiths managed to produce some extremely elegant models, some with the mechanism entirely concealed within the lockplate, others with it partly concealed and with the exposed portions heavily decorated. Indeed, the lock seems to have had a fascination out of all proportion to its utility, since it was manufactured (though in smaller and smaller numbers) right up to the early years of the 19th century. Where mechanical elegance was demanded, the wheel-lock had a place.

The operation of the wheel-lock was, of course, very similar in its basic features to the common domestic action of striking sparks from a piece of flint by the application of a piece of steel – the basic method of obtaining fire used in the middle ages. And the flint, being a considerably harder stone than the iron pyrites used in the wheel-lock, was a more durable and attractive proposition if it could be made to function in a gun lock. Attempts to replace the pyrites with flint were not successful, since the flint was so hard that it soon ruined the teeth of the wheel, so another line of approach was needed.

17th CENTURY ENGLISH SNAPHAUNCE REVOLVER

This interesting attempt to produce a multishot weapon suffered from the inherent instability of all black-powder guns. The ignition of the priming charge for one cylinder could set off all the charges which generally meant that the firer lost his hand in the resulting explosion. Like later multishot weapons this snaphaunce revolver was reliable when the working parts were new and unworn. However, the presence of black powder unprotected by any form of cartridge would remain an insoluble hazard until the late 19th century

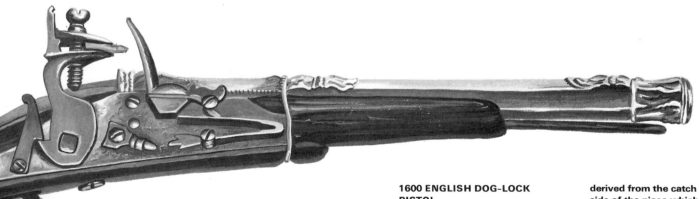

1600 ENGLISH DOG-LOCK PISTOL

This pistol has a steel mechanism, but a brass barrel. The use of 'soft' metals was quite practical since the forces exerted by the main charge were comparatively low and depended on the load of powder and ball that suited the firer. The name 'dog' was derived from the catch on the side of the piece which locked the pistol in a half-cock position when the cock was thumbed back. This example of a dog-lock pistol has the popular club like grip suitable for use in close combat. Locks for handguns were developed throughout Europe using different configurations

WHEEL-LOCK TO FLINTLOCK

The flintlock made its appearance in about the middle of the 16th century, though its exact place of birth is in some doubt. It seems probable that, like so many inventions, the same idea occurred to different people in different places at much the same time, and there are certainly two distinct streams of development of the flintlock, which eventually merge and divide again to provide five different and distinct types of lock.

The first was probably the Spanish lock or 'miquelet', of which there is documentary record as early as 1547. Whether it was a purely Spanish invention, or whether it was developed in Italy and perfected in Spain, is a question unlikely ever to be settled, but its development is commonly attributed to Simon Marquarte, the son of a similarly-named Italian lockmaker who had gone to Spain at the invitation of the Emperor Charles.

The miquelet lock consisted of a 'cock' with jaws which gripped a shaped piece of flint, and a 'frizzen', an angled steel plate which acted to cover the priming pan and also intercepted the travel of the flint. The cock was propelled by a powerful leaf spring acting on its heel to force it forward. To prepare the weapon the cock was pulled back against the spring until a cross-bolt, or 'sear' moved across the frame of the lock and came to rest beneath the toe of the cock and thus locked it in place. The frizzen was hinged forward and powder sprinkled into the pan, and the frizzen then closed again to hold the powder in the pan and protect it against moisture. When the trigger was pulled, the sear was withdrawn, allowing the cock to fly forward. As the cock, carrying the flint, moved down, so the flint struck the flat face of the frizzen; this had two results, firstly to strike sparks, and secondly, due to the angle of fall, to knock the frizzen out of the way, hinging it forward, to expose the powder in the pan so that the sparks could fall into the pan and ignite the powder.

One notable feature of the Spanish lock was that there were two sears, one below the other, and the cock could be drawn back less than the full distance so as to rest on the second sear, a position which came to be known as half-cock. The mechanism was arranged so that this half cock sear could not be withdrawn by the trigger until the cock was brought fully back and held by the main sear, so that the half-cock position became a form of safety catch. Moreover, the mechanical advantage of the mainspring was such that even if it were possible to fire from the half-cock position, the force generated by the falling cock would probably be insufficient to strike spark or open the frizzen.

At much the same period, the Dutch 'snaphaunce' lock made its appearance. The differences between the Spanish and Dutch locks are matters of detail rather than of principle, since the basic features of the cock, frizzen and pan are still there. But on the Dutch lock the mainspring acts on the toe of the cock while the sear acts on the heel, directly opposite to the Spanish arrangement. Moreover, the Dutch frizzen acts only as a spark producer and does not double as a cover to the priming pan. The pan is closed by a separate sliding lid which is linked to the cock by a rod; as the cock swings forward so the rod is pushed forward and slides the pan cover clear to allow the sparks, struck from the frizzen, to fall inside. Another significant difference was that the Spanish lock mounted its mainspring on the outside of the

SPANISH MIQUELET

The miquelet with its cock and frizzen was an important step on the way to the flintlock. The frizzen covered the pan and was hinged forward when the firer was about to discharge the piece, the cock with a sliver of flint screwed between its jaws being held under tension by a leaf spring. A sear held the cock in position and when the trigger was pulled it was withdrawn, to allow the cock to fly forward and strike the frizzen producing a spark which ignited the powder in the pan

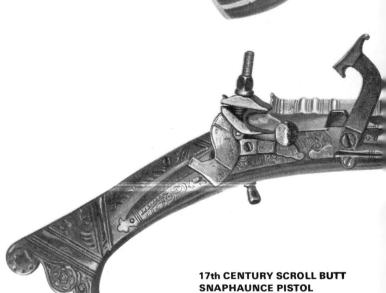

17th CENTURY SCROLL BUTT SNAPHAUNCE PISTOL

This Scottish pistol with its brass barrel and steel working parts has a steel rod beneath the barrel for ramming the powder, ball and wadding. Preparing a black powder piece took time and in battle soldiers sometimes forgot to remove the ramrod before they fired. This not only rendered the piece inoperable since it could not be reloaded, but also made an unusual but not very effective projectile. In most armies the loss of a ramrod was regarded as a very serious offence

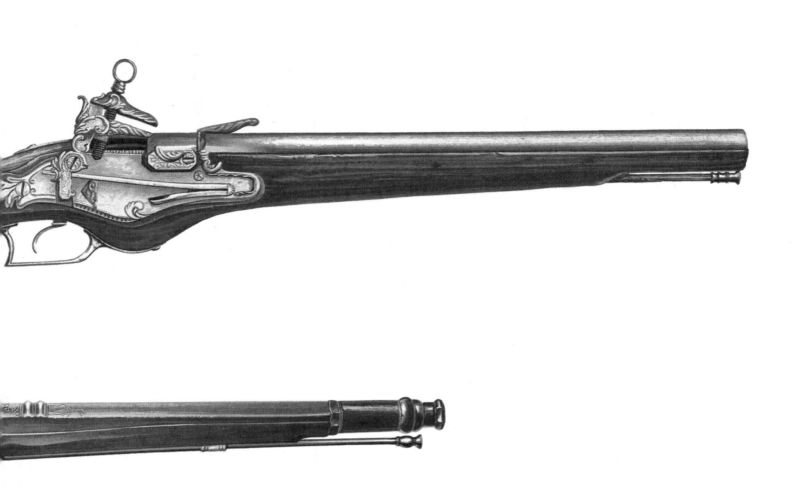

A 17th century marksman takes aim during a competition to 'shoot the popinjay'. The popinjay was a mark in the shape of a bird. Given the rudimentary nature of weapons in the 17th century, ranges for sporting and military shooting would have been very short. In practice the handgun gave a man the ability to stand off from an enemy and kill or disable him before he could be clubbed or run through

POCKET PISTOL BY DURS EGG, LONDON 1700

This tidy little weapon, attractively inlaid and blued, was produced as personal protection for travellers. The heavy horse pistols in their saddle-mounted buckets were too large to be carried comfortably in a coat pocket but pocket pistols were light and effective at short ranges. The flintlock mechanism was sufficiently compact to allow pocket weapons to be designed and carried cocked and ready for action with a reasonable degree of safety to their owners. This pistol has a bone tipped ramrod which reduces the danger of friction between the barrel and the rod when tamping down the powder

Fotomas Index

SPANISH MIQUELET PISTOL, 1690

This beautiful pistol with its inlay and engraving shows how handguns were still the preserve of the wealthy even in the late 17th century. Combining art and utility in weapons with engraving and high quality wood grips is still continued by a few gunsmiths, but the demand for vast numbers of firearms for conscript armies has put an emphasis on utility

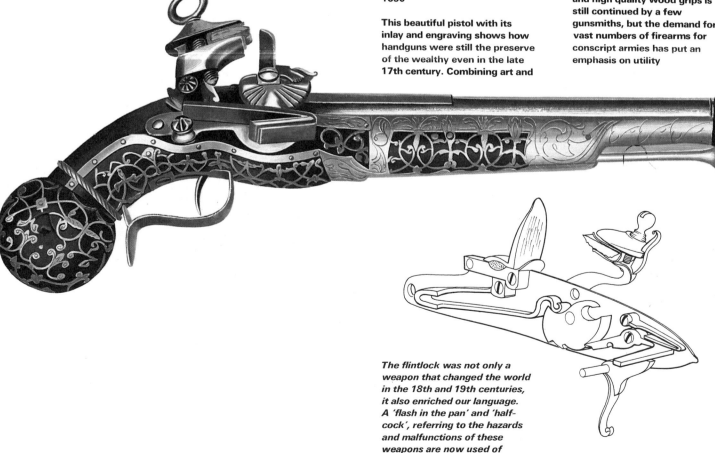

The flintlock was not only a weapon that changed the world in the 18th and 19th centuries, it also enriched our language. A 'flash in the pan' and 'half-cock', referring to the hazards and malfunctions of these weapons are now used of events or people

Displaying an uncommonly high standard of horsemanship, Dick Turpin, the English highwayman, clears a spiked toll gate during his epic ride to York. He is armed with two heavy flintlock pistols, one of which is in use to deter the toll collector

THE FLINTLOCK MECHANISM

This fairly simple method of initiating a charge in a pistol, musket or rifle could be mass-produced to arm the conscript armies of the Napoleonic wars. A peasant soldier could be trained quickly and easily how to operate a musket

lock plate, where it could be easily repaired, while the Dutch mounted their spring on the inside of the lock where it was better protected against dirt and damage.

As might be expected, once the snap-lock had made its mark the idea spread and led to some variations. The English lock, or 'dog-lock' appears to have been derived from the Dutch snaphaunce. This lock takes its name from the addition of a small hook, or 'dog', on the side of the frame behind the cock. On pulling back the cock this dog snapped into a recess on the cock so as to hold it at the half-cock position. It was quite impossible to release the cock by pulling the trigger, since the dog was not linked to the trigger in any way. The only way to fire the gun was to pull back the cock to the fully-cocked position, then thumb the dog out of the way before pressing the trigger. The other main change in the English lock was the adoption of the Spanish idea of making the frizzen and pan cover in one piece. Apart from that, the basic layout was as the Dutch, with the mainspring concealed within the lock plate.

The Swedish lock used a long and slender cock which appears to have been descended from the form used in the matchlock, and which gives these locks a most distinctive form. The separate frizzen of the Dutch lock was used, but the pan cover, while separate and sliding, was not mechanically linked to the cock but had to be opened just before firing by the firer himself. The mechanism was extremely simple, there being no half-cock refinements, and the spring was concealed within the lock plate.

Finally, after considering the features of these four locks, the French perfected the mechanism into the final flintlock design, the French lock. Their first attempt resembled the Dutch snaphaunce lock, though it rarely featured the inter-connecting rod which opened the pan, relying on the firer opening it manually. The principal innovation was the provision of a shaped cam, known as the 'tumbler' inside the lock and on the pivot around which the cock revolved. The tumbler was provided with notches for full and half cock, and also with a notch for the engagement of the main spring to provide the necessary power to the cock.

This model was merely a step in the right direction, though, and was soon superseded by the perfected type which eventually became the accepted standard for flintlocks throughout the world. In this final model the French went back to the miquelet lock of Spain and took the one-piece frizzen and pan cover, shaping it more carefully to provide sound ignition and certain opening. Together with the tumbler, the new frizzen ensured that the resulting lock was as fool-proof and reliable as could be possibly wished, and from its inception in about 1635 to the end of the flintlock era two hundred years later, there was very little improvement to be found.

The principal advantages of the flintlock over the wheel-lock were firstly its reliability – there was less to go wrong; secondly its ease of maintenance, since flints were a good deal more easy to obtain and a good deal more durable than the soft iron pyrites of the wheel-lock; and thirdly its cheapness, since it was vastly simpler in its mechanical arrangements and much easier and quicker to make. Adoption of the flintlock meant that whole armies could now be provided with firearms of better quality than the old matchlock but at less expense than would have been the case with the wheel-lock.

And, to return to the main theme once more, it was the flintlock which turned the pistol into a commonplace and inexpensive weapon. While it was possible for a master gunsmith to make a flintlock which was a thing of beauty and grace, it was equally possible for a competent blacksmith to make one which, for all it lacked in grace, worked equally well. And because there was this divergence of manufacture and because there was a wide variety of people wanting pistols for a wide variety of purposes, different patterns began to emerge, of pistols suited to different roles.

As might be expected the first to use the flintlock pistol in any numbers were the military, and it became a standard accoutrement of the cavalry trooper. Most of these cavalry pistols were heavy, of about .50- .65-in calibre and with barrels about a foot long. They were generally stocked to the muzzle, and the butt was finished with a heavy metal ornament, so that in extremis the weapon could be reversed and used as a club with good effect. The lock, on the right

side, was matched by a side-plate on the left side of the pistol, and the mainspring was concealed inside the lock plate while the frizzen spring was exposed beneath the pan.

The civilian equivalent of the cavalry pistol was the holster or 'horse' pistol, the names reflecting the fact that the pistols were of such a size that they needed to be carried in holsters and the holsters needed to be carried on horseback. The hip-mounted holster was a long way in the future, and the holster was more akin to the 'bucket' in which the cavalryman carried his carbine or long pistol. The general style was much the same as that of the military pistol but, since they were not standardised and were the products of individual gunmakers with a reputation to sustain, most of them were decorated or ornamented to a greater or lesser degree. Lock plates were chiselled with relief designs, sideplates became ornate carvings of metal, frequently in silver, the butt cap was usually a lions head or a grotesque mask, the trigger guard finished with an ornamental finial, the ramrod furnished with

a decorated finger grip and so forth. From this the decoration extended to inletting gold and silver into the stock to produce fine designs, and eventually the barrel became a vehicle for the decorator's art. The limit to decoration appears to have been little more than the amount of money the buyer was prepared to lay out, to the point where some pistols were so decorated that they were no longer feasible as weapons.

A smaller cousin of the holster pistol was the type known as the 'travelling pistol' from its adoption by men whose business required them to travel about in coaches. The sword was of no use in the confined space of a coach, should the vehicle be stopped by a highwayman (armed, of course, with a brace of holster pistols) but a pair of travelling pistols could be carried inside the coach in an inconspicuous case ready loaded, and produced when the need arose.

A special variety of the military pistol was the 'Scottish' pistol. As the name implies they were made by Scots gunsmiths, but there is more to it than that; they were a unique design, instantly recognisable and identifiable and impossible to confuse with any other contemporary pistol. The most readily visible feature of the Scottish pistol is that (with a very few early exceptions) they are entirely made of metal instead of employing the usual form of wooden stockbutt. Iron was commonly used, though brass stocks are not unknown, and the metal was ornamented and formed into a variety of shapes for the termination of the butt; lemons, hearts and rams horns were some of the most popular designs which were used as ornamentation.

The second feature marking the Scottish pistol is the absence of any form of trigger guard, the trigger being formed into a knob or ball decoration. And the third feature is the presence of a ball, matching the trigger, at the bottom of the butt; this is the handle of a vent-clearing pricker screwed into the butt so as to be readily available for reaming out the vent between pan and chamber should it become fouled with powder residue.

HEAVY FLINTLOCK BLUNDERBUSS PISTOL, CLARK AND SON, LONDON 1790

The blunderbuss with its bell shaped barrel could be loaded with a lethal mix of lead shot and small scrap. It was often carried on mail coaches or used by rural householders in the 18th century. The blunderbuss may seem a rather ridiculous weapon designed to give the poor shot a chance of hitting a fleeting target. However it was a particularly deadly piece which had an effect like grape shot at short ranges. The mix of shot to propellant could be adjusted according to the owners needs or taste

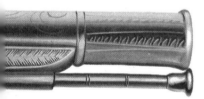

EARLY 19th-CENTURY ALL-STEEL SCOTTISH PISTOL WITH RAMSHORN BUTT

These pistols are readily recognisable by their all-metal design and lack of trigger guard. The butt has a vent clearing pricker for reaming out the vent between the pan and the chamber when it became clogged with powder residue after several shots. An all-steel weapon was more durable than wood and brass pistols, but required a very high standard of workmanship to finish off the hot forged parts

A pistol-armed highwayman rides down his victim on a winter afternoon

Mansell Collection

Duelling – pistols at dawn

Probably no pistol of the flintlock era strikes the imagination so much as the duelling pistol, though in truth, most of the pistols so described are not duelling weapons at all. The duel had been a feature of aristocratic life for centuries, but in the middle of the 17th century the pistol began to supersede the sword as the chosen instrument. It may well have been that the pistol was felt to bring an equalising element to the combat, since there were innumerable examples of highly-skilled swordsmen slicing up unskilled opponents in extremely one-sided affairs. But even if this were the case, the balance was soon to be tilted in favour of the experienced duellist by virtue of his providing himself with a highly specialised pistol.

The code of the duel varied from place to place and from time to time, but generally speaking the rule was that the two parties stood back to back, paced out a certain distance, turned about and immediately fired, the taking of a deliberate aim being felt to be unsporting and being forbidden. It follows from this that the prime virtues in a pistol were firstly that the weapon should 'point' naturally; as soon as the holder raised it, instinctively pointing his hand at the target, so the pistol should fit and balance so that the barrel became an extension of the firer's arm and aligned itself perfectly with his opponent. The second requirement was that the trigger should be light and fast in operation, and to this end the locks of duelling pistols were carefully fitted and the springs lightened as much as possible consistent with reliable action; the slightest pressure of the finger was enough to discharge the pistol. This, of course, worked both ways; when the challenger offered his matched pair of pistols to his opponent, who took one, the odds were that unless the opponent was used to a hair-trigger he would inadvertently fire the weapon while he was still in the process of aiming it. This would result in a miss, and the other party could then be quite sure of himself before he fired.

Contrary to general belief, the duelling pistol was rarely ornamented beyond a few scrolls on the lock plate and on the butt cap, while the butt was checked to provide a perfect grip. The inside of the barrel was carefully polished, while the outside was browned or blued so as not to reflect light which might dazzle or distract the firer. In similar cause, silver and brass fittings and ornamentation were foresworn. In an attempt to put weight into the barrel and thus aid pointing, it became the practice to terminate the wooden stock just ahead of the trigger guard but to stiffen the barrel by forging a rib beneath it to give both strength and weight.

One of the last refinements to appear on the duelling pistol was the 'saw handle' grip, in which the wood of the stock was shaped to fit over the thumb-web of the firer's hand. This sort of grip ensures that the hand and the gun are always in the same relative position, and the firer will always grip the pistol in the same way. Thus, once sufficiently practiced with the weapon, it literally became an extension of his arm and missing was well-nigh impossible.

'Slugs in a sawpit'; a Rowlandson cartoon showing how crude duelling could become when two men were bent on avenging their highly protected 'honour'

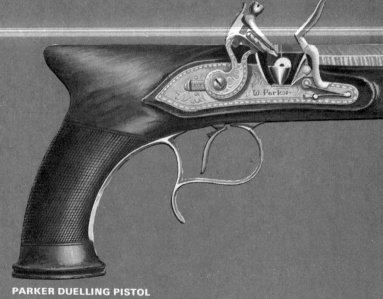

PARKER DUELLING PISTOL 1815

Duelling pistols were exceptional weapons made for one purpose – a single accurate shot. They were therefore given a light, fast trigger and designed to 'point' naturally in the firer's hand. This Parker pistol has a trigger guard and grip which fit comfortably and easily into the average hand

The Duke of Wellington takes aim at Lord Winchelsea during the duel over the Catholic Relief Bill for Ireland on March 21, 1829. Though the Duke of Wellington appears to be intent on hitting his victim both men aimed to miss during the duel. Wellington did not approve of duelling and during the Peninsula War issued an order banning duels because he had lost a number of young officers

Peter Newark's Western Americana

A FRENCH DUELLING PISTOL

The duelling pistol was notable for its lack of embellishments. The barrel was blued or browned to reduce glare when the duellist came into the aim. The interior of the barrel however was carefully polished. The use of rifled barrels was regarded as unsporting in Britain since the aim of the duel was to satisfy honour and this did not necessarily require death. Though duelling was practised in Britain it was often regarded as a continental vice

DUCK'S FOOT AND PEPPERBOX

So far the pistols we have considered have all been muzzle-loading types, requiring to be loaded with powder, wad and ball, rammed down, and the pan then primed with fine powder. But as early as the 15th century breech-loading weapons had been produced; not very successfully, it is true, but the idea was there and gunsmiths never gave up trying to find a method of loading which would be less trouble and which would give more regular ballistics. In the middle of the 17th century came the 'turn-off' pistol, which appeared to provide what was wanted. Basically it was a flintlock pistol in which the barrel was a separate component, screwed on to the breech end of the weapon. Thus to load, the barrel was unscrewed and removed – or turned off – and the chamber, which remained attached to the butt and lock section, was filled with powder; since the chamber was a finite size it would be filled always to the same level, thus ensuring regularity of the charge weight. The ball could then be dropped into the breech end of the barrel, and since it did not have to be rammed down from the muzzle, it could be a much better fit. The barrel was then screwed back on to the breech, the pan primed, and the pistol was ready. To some degree this was a more fiddling performance than muzzle loading, and so the turn-off pistol never achieved much prominence in military circles, where the loading drill was well practised and brought to a fine art. In some designs of pistol the barrel was encircled with a loose ring which was hooked to the body of the pistol so that there was no danger of accidentally dropping the barrel in the haste of loading.

The design of the turn-off pistol soon led to a characteristic shape appearing. It was obviously awkward to have a fully-stocked pistol if it was intended to unscrew the barrel for every shot, and thus the wooden stock was the first thing to go. The breech end was swelled out and frequently made octagonal or otherwise angular so that it could be gripped by a spanner in the event of the barrel choosing to stick tight, and the rear end of the barrel was similarly shaped for the same reason. As a result of this shaping, the barrel flowed into the stock, without any woodwork protruding forward of the trigger guard, and the frizzen spring was carefully changed so as to extend backwards beneath the pan instead of forwards alongside the barrel, where it would have interfered with the application of a spanner.

Since this form of construction removed the support of the stock from the generally-thin barrel, the barrel itself was changed, and given reinforcing rings, particularly at the muzzle, so that it resembled the contemporary cannon. This, in turn, led to the term 'cannon-barrelled' for this type of pistol. Another name frequently used is 'Queen Anne', though in fact most of the pistols of this form appeared after that monarch's time.

A last improvement in this type of pistol was to move the position of the lock. This was a fundamental change, because ever since the matchlock the mechanism had been hung on a lock plate on the right hand side of the weapon. But with the more graceful form of the turn-off pistol, particularly in small calibres for carrying in the pocket, the positioning of the cock and frizzen on the outside of the pistol made an inconvenient handful. So the lock was redesigned and moved into the centre-line of the weapon. The pan was formed at the end of the breech, with the frizzen immediately above it, and the

cock and its mechanism was fitted into the centre of the butt stock, boxed in on either side by metal sideplates. Since the earlier model had been on the side of the gun it became known as the 'side lock', and the new design became the 'box lock'.

Introducing the bullet from the rear end of the barrel allowed another old principle to be applied more commonly, that of rifling. Rifled barrels had long been known, and employed on long arms, but in pistols they were less common, since the necessity to force the ball down the barrel and into the rifling was more difficult to achieve in a pistol. With a rifled musket, the butt could be rested on the ground and the ball driven in with the loader's full strength, even using a mallet to start it if necessary, but trying to do this with a pistol held in the hand was far from easy. Some duelling pistols employed rifled barrels, since loading them was a more deliberate affair, but the general run of flintlocks were smoothbored for simplicity's sake. The introduction of the turn-off barrel, however, allowed rifling to be employed, with a consequent gain in accuracy and regularity of performance. It is recorded that Prince Rupert, armed with two rifled turn-off pistols, entered Stafford on 13 September 1642 and, at a range of 60 yards, put a bullet through the weathercock of St Mary's Church. When his uncle, King Charles I, expressed amazement at the feat, Prince Rupert drew his other pistol and hit the weathercock again.

So far we have considered what might be called conventional pistols, pistols with a lock and a single barrel. But there was no shortage of gunsmiths ready to experiment and produce unusual weapons, just as there was no shortage of people ready to try them out. The earliest variation was brought about by the natural desire to have more than one shot available in case the first one missed or in case there was more than one adversary to be dealt with. The double-barrelled pistol was the solution to this, and such weapons became fairly commonplace. They were no more than two single barrel units joined side-by-side, the only mechanical change being that one of the locks, obviously, had to be left-handed. But beyond that there was little mechanical novelty about them.

Somewhat more adventurous was the 'superimposed load' type of weapon, in which a single barrel was made to discharge several shots in quick succession. This was done using what is best described as a 'Roman Candle' principle; the pistol was charged with powder and bullet, then more powder, another bullet, more powder, another bullet and so on until six or eight shots were in place. Each bullet was pierced with a hole from front to back, this hole being filled with a delay composition, a slow-burning powder. The pistol was built with the lock much further forward than normal, with the vent opposite the foremost charge. When fired, the first charge exploded and expelled the first bullet. It also lit the delay composition in the bullet behind it, which then burned through and fired the second charge, shooting the second bullet out. This in turn lit the delay leading through bullet number three to fire charge number three, and so on until the gun was empty. With a suitably timed delay, an astute operator, and an agile hand, it would have been possible to spread the bullets around in quite lethal fashion with some practice. Unfortunately, there was also the danger that if the bullets were not a tight fit in the bore the flash

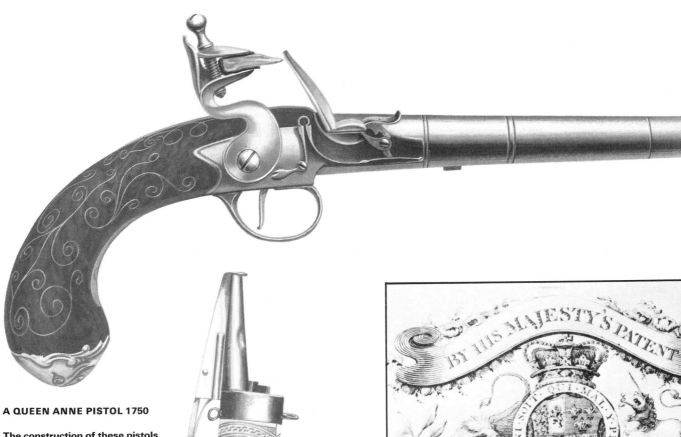

A QUEEN ANNE PISTOL 1750

The construction of these pistols used methods normally used with cannon. The result was that the barrel was lighter than earlier pistols, but reinforced with rings at intervals along its length. The name was strictly a misnomer since most of the pistols appeared after Queen Anne's death

EARLY 17th CENTURY ANTLER POWDER FLASK

The powder flask was a secure way of carrying gunpowder in the field. The neck was fitted with a spring loaded top which allowed the firer to control the flow of powder and prevent the entrance of damp. This attractive flask may have been for a hunting piece since the decoration and materials are not common with military arms

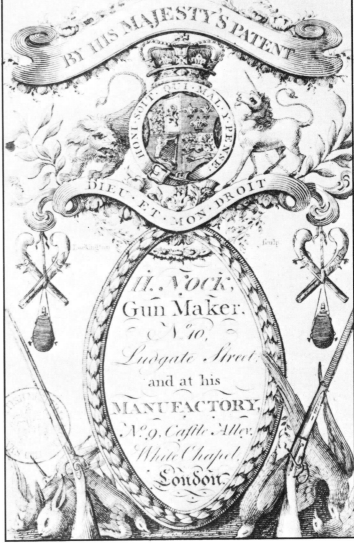

The gunmaker's label on the inside lid of a case for a pair of pistols

DUCK'S FOOT PISTOL .45-in CALIBRE

This was one of the many attempts to give one man sufficient fire-power to engage a gang at close range. The 'Mob Pistol' or 'Duck's Foot Pistol' had a lateral spread of 20-30° with each barrel loaded with a heavy lead slug. It had been designed for bank guards as protection against footpads, but was popular with prison guards and ship's captains

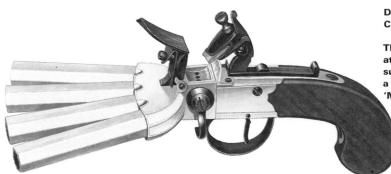

A SIX-BARRELLED .38-in CALIBRE FLINTLOCK BY BRASHER OF LONDON 1780

This tidy pistol shows the numbered barrels which could be unscrewed for loading. Like the Duck's Foot it required only one action to operate the trigger and fire all six barrels. Guns like this were not designed for the gentry and this is reflected in the simplicity and lack of embellishment

A 24-SHOT PEPPERBOX

The pepperbox offered the firer a chance to fire a succession of shots, but at first gunsmiths had not devised a method for rotating the barrels and the firer had to turn these by hand. However this was a great improvement on one-shot multi-barrel pistols and was another step on the way to the pistol with a revolving cylinder

could leak down the side of bullet two and ignite all the charges at once, with disastrous results.

A slight refinement of this system was to insert a solid bullet into the chain; once the charge in front of this had been fired, the chain reaction would stop since there was no way for the next charge to be lit. This type of pistol had a sliding lock, which could now be moved back to a second vent, opposite the unfired front charge, with the second pan primed the pistol could be fired a second time to deliver a second string of bullets.

Although these 'Roman Candle' guns appeared from time to time from the middle 1600s to the middle 1800s, they were never very popular, probably because one could never be quite sure what the result would be when the trigger was pressed. A more practical system for sharing out the contents of a pistol among many recipients was the 'Mob Pistol' or, as it is more commonly known, the 'Duck's Foot Pistol'. This had the usual lock and breech piece of a turn-off pistol but screwed to the breech piece is a block which, in turn, had four or more barrels screwed into it, each set at an angle so that some 20 or 30° of lateral spread was obtained. One charge was used, in the breech piece, but each barrel was loaded with its own ball, so that on firing four or five separate bullets flew out. It is said to have been originally developed for bank guards so that they could deal with gangs of footpads, but they are also reputed to have found favour with prison guards and with ship's captains, who must have found a pair of them comforting when confronted with a mutinous crew and it was not necessary to pick an individual target.

Equally formidable, though less-widely-spread in its effect, was the four-barrelled pistol in which the four barrels were simply forged in a single block which replaced the usual

LORENZONI-TYPE REPEATING PISTOL 1790

Designed by Michael Lorenzoni this pistol worked by cranking a lever on the left side. This deposited a load of powder, then a ball, cocked the cock and then primed the pan. Lorenzoni, who worked in Florence, had a disciple and competitor in a gunsmith called Berselli in Bologna

COLLIER FIVE-CHAMBERED FLINTLOCK 1820

This flintlock was more compact than a pepperbox, but it was still necessary to rotate the chambers and lock them into position, prime the pan and then, after cocking the action, the gun was ready to fire another shot

barrel. In this case each barrel had its own charge and bullet, the vent communicating with all four chambers so as to fire the bullets simultaneously.

Useful as these weapons might have been in dealing with a mob of attackers, they were of limited appeal; a more attractive idea was to have a pistol which could be loaded with several shots and then fired one shot at a time, as and when needed. The double-barrelled gun had this ability, of course, but in a limited fashion. A four-barrelled gun would be a good thing, but the prospect of trying to fit four locks on to a pistol was not an easy one. The solution came with the 'tap action' pistol in which a small tap (or faucet) could be turned to open or close the vents to the various barrels. Thus the first barrel could be fired and the tap turned to open the vent to barrel number two, after which the pan was reprimed and the weapon recocked. Another method of

reaching the same result was the pepperbox pistol, in which a number of barrels – usually six – were formed into a rotating unit in front of the lock. In the usual type the firer cocked the lock and primed the pan and then fired the first barrel. He then manually turned the cluster of barrels until the second barrel was in place, recocked, reprimed, and fired again. Some pepperboxes carried a separate pan for each barrel, fitted with a tightly sprung frizzen, so that all the barrels could be primed beforehand and the six barrels could be fired as fast as the firer could recock and rotate the barrels. Some gunsmiths took the matter a stage further by arranging a linkage so that as the cock was drawn back, so the barrel cluster was rotated the necessary amount, though this refinement was uncommon. The idea was sound enough as long as the gun was new, but as soon as wear developed in the frizzens and springs, the shock of firing the first barrel

BREECH-LOADING PISTOL ON THE PAULY SYSTEM

This pistol, made by Joseph Manton in 1820, used compressed air as a propellant. This had the advantage of producing no flash or smoke but was underpowered. Most air-guns were either too cumbersome for practical use or if light enough to be carried they fired a very modest projectile

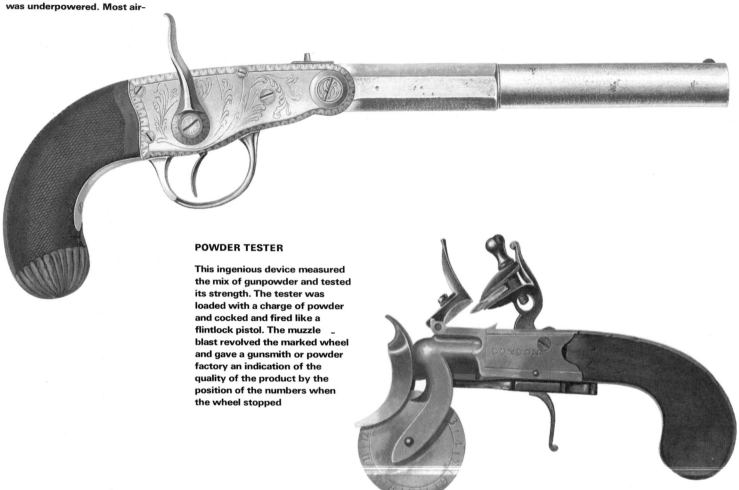

POWDER TESTER

This ingenious device measured the mix of gunpowder and tested its strength. The tester was loaded with a charge of powder and cocked and fired like a flintlock pistol. The muzzle blast revolved the marked wheel and gave a gunsmith or powder factory an indication of the quality of the product by the position of the numbers when the wheel stopped

could easily jar open the frizzens of some of the other barrels and throw their priming out on the ground, to the distress of the firer when he suffered a misfire on the third or fourth shot.

By the beginning of the 19th century the flintlock had reached a very highly perfected state, but even so it was a long way from being the perfect method of discharging a firearm. In the first place the contact of flint and steel caused the flint to be chipped away slightly at every shot, and after 30 or 40 shots it was necessary to remove the flint and replace it, or at the least, reface the flint to produce a fresh striking edge. Neglect of this led to misfires; one official test of flintlocks indicated that the average was one misfire for every 38 successful shots. Another grave disadvantage was that due to the construction of the breech, with the vent set off to one side, ignition of the charge was uncertain. What happened was that the flame came down the vent and lit that portion of the charge in close promimity to the end of the vent, from which ignition spread to the remainder of the charge. The odds were that the ball would have started up the bore before the entire charge was lit, and the subsequent rapid fluctuations of pressure could play havoc with the potential accuracy of the weapon. Several gunsmiths appreciated this point and evolved complex cures; vents which curved beneath the barrel to come up beneath the centre of the charge; vents which communicated with the rear end of the barrel to light the charge centrally; auxiliary chambers which fired first and then lit the main charge. But none of these were particularly successful and all of them required intricate manufacture and were wide open to problems with fouling.

Another problem was in the time delay between pulling the trigger and having the gun go off; there were distinct steps in the chain of events which could be discerned without much trouble. First the hammer fell and struck sparks from the frizzen; then the powder in the pan fired; and then the charge exploded and the bullet was ejected. Unaided eyesight was sufficient to distinguish these steps; there was no need for instrumentation. The result of this showed itself in two distinct fields. In the military field it meant that the recruit had to be carefully trained to avoid flinching when the priming fired and maintain his aim until his musket or pistol went off. The official manual *Exercise of the Firelock*, in force at the beginning of the 19th century, made this quite clear: "The recruit having acquired the habit of aligning the firelock with any object selected by the eye, he will next be taught to burn priming without winking or in the slightest degree altering the composure of his contenance. . . . The instructor must watch the recruit minutely in this practice, which must be continued until the eye is perfectly indifferent

COPPER POWDER FLASK

The powder horn or flask remained in use for long after the introduction of cartridges. It was used by wild fowlers and hunters armed with muzzle-loaders or punt guns who needed a controlled flow of gunpowder for loading their pieces

National Army Museum

to the flash caused by the ignition of the powder. . . ."

In the civilian field, hunters were complaining that the flash of the priming frequently scared the bird or beast so that it moved before the ball had time to reach it. One such hunter was the Reverend Alexander Forsyth, of Belhelvie, a few miles from Aberdeen, who was extremely annoyed by the advance warning given to the local birds by the fizzing of the priming in his shotgun. Like so many men of his time, Forsyth was an amateur scientist and he began devoting his time to the development of some faster and more certain method of firing the charge.

In 1800 Edward Charles Howard announced his discovery of mercury fulminate, a chemical compound which, when struck a light blow, detonated. It was (and still is for that matter) a highly dangerous material, and Howard was to be severely injured in the course of his experiments. The Reverend Forsyth saw possibilities in this new material, but used alone it was far too violent and sensitive. After some years of research and experiment Forsyth developed a mixture of mercury fulminate and potassium chlorate which was sufficiently sensitive to be set off by the fall of the flintlock-pattern cock but not so destructive as to damage the gun, and providing ample flash for igniting the charge. Moreover the more violent action of this mixture drove the ignition flash into the chamber in such a manner as to give far better

ignition to the gunpowder and thus more regularity to the shooting.

This was all very well, but in order to make use of this material a suitable lock had to be designed, and Forsyth worked at this until he eventually took out a patent in 1807. Basically his lock was the mechanism of a flintlock, but instead of the cock carrying a flint in a pair of jaws, it merely carried a suitably shaped hammer-head. In place of the pan and frizzen was a hollow bolt leading into the gun chamber and, riding on the bolt, a tubular magazine which could be twisted around its vertical axis. To operate the gun, this magazine was first filled with the 'detonating powder'; it was then twisted through 180°, which deposited a small quantity of powder in the tube leading to the vent; the magazine was then twisted back, so that the powder-carrying section was moved out of the way and a solid section, carrying only a short rod, sat above the vent and the small priming charge. When the trigger was pressed, the cock fell and struck the top of the rod; this, driven down, impacted on the detonating composition and fired it, so that the flash went into the chamber and fired the gun. No fizzle, no delay; the birds of Belhelvie had very little time to be surprised before they were in the Reverend's bag. Legend has it that Napoleon offered Forsyth £20000 for the secret of his invention, prior to his taking out a patent, but Forsyth patriotically refused it.

Whatever the truth of that may be, it is certainly a fact that in 1805 he set out for London and the Master-General of the Ordnance, in order to give the British Army the benefit of his discovery. Lord Moira, the Master-General, was impressed and gave Forsyth facilities in the armoury of the Tower of London, but at that time the idea was far from perfect and a year's work still did not result in a reliable lock. A new Master-General was appointed who had no sympathy with the idea and peremptorily called on Forsyth to remove his 'rubbish' from the Tower and be gone. He duly went, and allied himself with James Watt, the celebrated engineer. With Watt's assistance he successfully applied for the patent which covered almost every possible application of fulminate for gun priming, set up a company in London to manufacture locks and guns, and then returned to his flock in Belhelvie. It should be added that, in course of time, the military adopted the Forsyth principle and he was eventually awarded £200 in 1840 – a sum which was far less than he had expended out of his own pocket in the course of his experiments in the Tower. He died in 1843, and after some public outcry over the scurvy treatment that had been meted out to him, he was posthumously awarded a further £1000.

The original form of Forsyth lock was soon replaced by an improved model which, due to its shape, has gone down in history as the 'scent bottle lock'. Instead of a magazine revolving in the vertical axis, the scent bottle revolved around the end of the vent. It performed the same function, though; the magazine was loaded with detonating powder, the hammer (a new name for the cock, because it 'hammered' the fulminate) was drawn back, and the scent bottle revolved base uppermost. This deposited a measured amount of powder into the vent. The bottle was then revolved until the other end was uppermost, this end carrying a pin which now rested above the powder, while the powder remaining in the magazine was carefully isolated from the area of the vent. Pulling the trigger dropped the hammer onto the pin, the pin struck the powder, and the gun fired. The scent bottle could hold sufficient powder for about 30 shots. Subsequent improvements of the lock linked the hammer with the bottle so that pulling back the hammer automatically drew the magazine back and deposited a charge of fulminate, while pulling the trigger dropped the hammer and also moved the magazine forward so as to present the pin to the hammer as it arrived at the lock.

Forsyth's lock enjoyed some success, and near-copies were soon in production by other makers throughout Europe. But it was a troublesome device, requiring filling with powder, and needing to be carefully maintained so that it metered out the right amount whenever it was operated. Some easier method was needed, and one which did not require the complexities of the magazine. Two solutions appeared at about the same time, around the year 1815. One was the percussion tube, invented by Joseph Manton, a famous English gunsmith. This was a thin copper tube containing the fulminate composition, inserted into the vent so that one end was exposed. The hammer fell on to this exposed end and detonated the composition, and the tube directed the flame into the gun chamber. It worked well enough, but removing the tube from the vent was not an easy task. A far better idea was the percussion cap which appears to have occurred to several people at about the same time. Manton and another

English gunsmith Joseph Egg are said to have developed it in England, while a Captain Shaw patented the idea in America in 1814, and various Continental names have also been put forward as having had the same idea at much the same time.

The percussion cap can be likened to a small top hat in section, with the crown of the hat being lined with detonating composition. The pistol (or, for that matter, any other arm) was made with a tubular extension from the vent, called the 'nipple', carefully made so that the cap could be pressed on to it making a snug fit. The hammer fell so as to crush the top of the cap, hammering the composition into contact with the top of the nipple, generating a flash which then passed through the nipple and vent into the chamber of the gun to fire the charge. The hammer was usually made with a recessed head which enclosed the cap at the moment of impact, so as to prevent fragments of copper, split off by the explosion, from flying out and possibly injuring the shooter. After firing, the hammer was cocked and the remains of the cap removed from the top of the nipple.

While the percussion cap was struggling to gain acceptance there was no shortage of inventors attempting to promote other ideas. One such was the 'pill lock', which, like the cap, was aimed at doing away with the business of using loose detonating powder. In this system the powder was compressed into pills and the gun vent ended in a small pan or receptacle just big enough to take one pill. The hammer fell and fired the pill to flash down the vent. An advance on this was a repeating pill lock in which a mechanism something akin to Forsyth's scent bottle could be operated with every stroke of the hammer to drop a pill into the pan from a supply carried in the magazine.

One unusual variation on the pill lock came from a London gunsmith called Hewson; he placed the pill magazine in the head of the hammer and, by means of a ratchet, arranged it so that as the hammer was cocked the rotary magazine block turned and placed a new pill opposite an aperture. When the hammer fell this aperture dropped over the nipple, so that the pill was struck and the flash went from the hammer into the vent. It was, like so many of these notions, very sound when the gun was new, but once the magazine block began to wear, there was always the danger that the flash from the pill would spread around inside the magazine and detonate all the other pills at the same time.

Although these systems for rapid repriming of the gun were ingenious, they were largely superfluous since it didn't matter how fast you could reprime the lock if you still had to upend the pistol and muzzle-load it. Nevertheless, the mechanical devices developed by these early gunmakers were useful exercises, and they were to find some use in later years when methods of breech loading began to speed up the whole of the reloading cycle. The first pistols to adopt the new percussion system were single shot weapons which were, to all intents and purposes, flintlocks with a few modifications. Instead of the pan and frizzen, a nipple protruded from the side or centre of the breech, and instead of the cock there was now a hammer with a recessed face. Indeed, the rest of the weapon was so little changed that many gunsmiths made a successful living by simply taking the pan, frizzen and cock off a flintlock, fitting a nipple and a hammer, and thus converting the weapon to the new system at minimal cost to the owner.

ENGLISH PISTOL WITH FORSYTH LOCK

This pistol has a scent bottle primer which was given a half turn to deposit a small quantity of fulminate of mercury in the vent. The bottle was spring loaded and so returned to an upright position after the pistol had been primed. To load the bottle the screws were undone at the bottom and the fulminate of mercury poured in. Forsyth's invention introduced 'the hammer', for the old flintlock cock had become a hammer which crushed the detonating powder

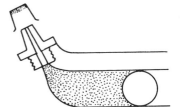

The percussion cap principle; the cap was fitted over a nipple and when struck exploded sending burning gases down to the powder charge in the barrel. It did away with clumsy flints and priming charges and was a step towards incorporating the percussion cap in a cartridge

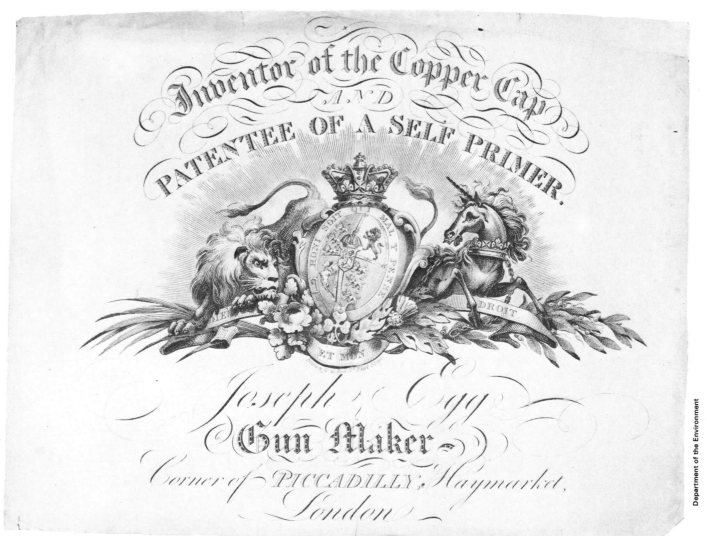

The label from a case of guns produced by Joseph Egg; the copper cap was the first step towards the self-priming cartridge and magazine fed pistols

ENTER THE REVOLVER

Gradually, though, new styles began to emerge, reflecting the changes in the world which wanted the gunsmiths' products. Among the earliest of the new classes of pistol was the tiny single-shot percussion weapon developed by one Henry Deringer of Philadelphia. Deringer had been a gunsmith for many years, making fine rifles and shotguns and also busy with military contracts, but around 1825 he turned to pistol making. His first attempts were quite conventional in size and form, but then he realised that there was a vast, new, and untouched market; America was expanding, there was lawlessness on the frontiers, and almost every man felt safer when carrying a pistol. On the other hand, few wanted to burden themselves with the usual heavy pistol of the day, preferring to have something which they could conceal about their person but which could be brought into play very quickly when the need arose. Deringer furnished the very thing they needed when he produced a compact but effective single shot weapon. Some were nine or ten inches long, some were as short as four inches, and the short weapons outnumbered the long ones. The calibre ranged from about .33- .50-in, delivering a powerful impact at short range. As target or hunting weapons they were unthinkable, but as short-range personal protection weapons, they were lethal across the width of a table or bar-room. Deringer pistols were associated with a number of well-publicised shootings in the first half of the 19th century, though probably none of them has gone down in history with quite the impact of John Wilkes Booth's shooting of Abraham Lincoln with a Deringer.

Deringer's success soon led to a rash of imitations, since Deringer never bothered to attempt to protect his design by patent – wisely, since he probably would not have succeeded in obtaining protection. Pistols calling themselves Derringer, Beringer, Heringer and suchlike punning look-alike names abounded, but the genuine Deringer stood above them by virtue of its workmanship. Nevertheless, in the century and a half which has gone by since Deringer first made his tiny pistol, his name, though often wrongly spelled, has attached itself to any single-shot heavy-bore short-barrel pistol, even though it may have been correctly applied only half the time.

Another pistol design which prospered briefly at this time was the under-hammer gun. The idea of putting the lock underneath the gun was not new; it had been flirted with in the flintlock period. The principal object seems to have been variously either to protect the pan and its contents from rain, or to produce a weapon of cleaner aspect and one which had an uncluttered top surface to allow easier aim and less likelihood of snagging it when withdrawing it from a holster.

The obvious objection to the design was that as soon as the cock struck the upside-down frizzen, the pan was opened and the powder fell out, but in practice it was found that the shower of sparks ignited the falling powder and the flash invariably went through the vent to fire the pistol. Even so, it was not exactly reliable, and the underhammer flint gun found few takers. But with the arrival of the percussion cap, the idea received a new boost, particularly in America, the result frequently being known as a 'boot' or even 'bootleg' pistol, since the lack of protruberant lock allowed it to be carried tucked into the top of a riding boot where it was readily accessible.

One of the most aberrant forms of pistol which appeared in

Library of Congress

John Wilkes Booth assassinates President Lincoln at Ford's theatre on 14 April, 1865. Booth used a Deringer pistol which was small and easy to conceal, but only effective at short ranges. Booth appears to have taken no chances with his weapon and carries a dagger in his left hand

COCHRAN'S .36-in CALIBRE TURRET GUN

This weapon, with charges loaded into chambers in the flat cylinder, offered the firer a hand portable multishot gun. Patented in 1837 it began to show defects after some use when the parts became worn. The flash from a detonating percussion cap could set off adjoining chambers and the others would follow in a series of sympathetic explosions. Since some of the chambers faced backwards the effect could be spectacular and in some cases fatal

Magazine: 7 shots

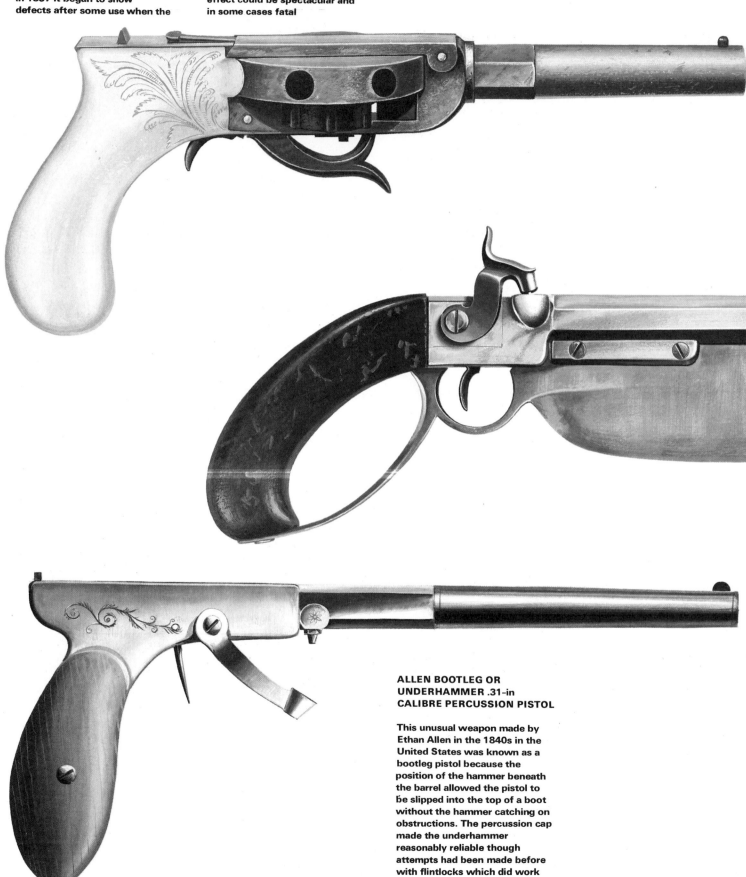

ALLEN BOOTLEG OR UNDERHAMMER .31-in CALIBRE PERCUSSION PISTOL

This unusual weapon made by Ethan Allen in the 1840s in the United States was known as a bootleg pistol because the position of the hammer beneath the barrel allowed the pistol to be slipped into the top of a boot without the hammer catching on obstructions. The percussion cap made the underhammer reasonably reliable though attempts had been made before with flintlocks which did work

ELGIN'S .38-in CALIBRE NAVY PISTOL/CUTLASS

Like earlier weapons this unusual configuration was designed to give a sailor in a boarding party a weapon which could be used in close combat after it had been discharged. The grip was protected by a guard and the 9-in blade had the added weight of the pistol behind it for slashing or thrusting. Patented in 1837 the pistol/cutlass did not enjoy a great success, perhaps because its bulk required a special holster to accommodate the blade and barrel. The US Navy equipped an expedition which sailed to the South Pacific in 1838 but when they returned in 1840 the designer and the manufacturers went bankrupt

DERINGER SINGLE-SHOT POCKET PISTOL

This single-shot pistol made by Henry Deringer of Philadelphia used a percussion cap. It was not intended for long range accuracy but rather as a life saver in a showdown in a bar or gaming saloon. Deringers came in a variety of calibres ranging from .33- .50-in

the early years of the percussion principle was the Elgin Cutlass Pistol, a single shot weapon with a 4-in long barrel, beneath which was forged a 9-in cutlass blade which extended about 5-in beyond the muzzle. Elgin patented this idea in 1837 and urged it on the United States Navy as a useful weapon for dealing with boarders and for use in the hand-to-hand fighting common in the naval warfare of that time. The navy were persuaded to buy 150 of them to outfit an expedition to the South Pacific in 1838, but by the time the expedition returned three years later, doubtless with a report on the efficacy of the pistol-cutlass, the designer was out of business and the manufacturers had gone bankrupt.

The prospect of firing several shots from one weapon still appealed, and, of course, the percussion system compared with the flintlock system made such designs more feasible. The usual two- and four-barrelled pistols, with and without the tap selector, duck's foot pistols, and pepperbox pistols all appeared with percussion locks, but in addition there were some new ideas afoot, to take advantage of the simpler lockwork needed.

The turret pistol was one early contender, and several designers appear to have hit on the idea at roughly the same time, the early 1830s. The system is best explained as a thick disc laid flat, behind the barrel of the pistol. Into the edge of the disc a number of chambers were bored, and leading from these, to either the upper or lower face of the disc, were vents which terminated in nipples. In some designs the disc could be removed, in others it was attached, but one way or another it was possible to load each separate chamber with powder and bullet and cap the nipples. The usual sort of hammer then fell when the trigger was pressed, to strike the cap relative to the chamber immediately behind the barrel, and discharge the load. What happened next depended upon the designer; in some it was necessary to move the turret round to line up the next chamber, while in others the movement was done automatically as the hammer was cocked for the next shot. Turret guns, both pistols and rifles, were produced by various makers and provided that they were well looked after they were serviceable enough. But when wear set in there was always the danger that the flame from the fired chamber might flash round and ignite one or more of the other chambers, or that the flash from one cap might touch off one or more of the others; in either case the result was spectacular, and could easily be fatal as the chambers erupted in all directions.

But the revolving principle seemed to be the right one, since it at least had the virtue of simplicity; the only thing at fault with the turret gun was the hazard of having one chamber pointed back towards the firer. Provided that all the chambers could be aligned so as to point in a safe direction, the revolver could be the chosen weapon. Plenty of people had made revolver-type arms in the wheel and flintlock periods, but, as might be imagined, they were more in the nature of technical exercises than practical weapons, ingenious designs which set out to pose the maker a problem and demonstrate his superiority in solving it. But again, the percussion system, with the simplicity of the hammer and nipple, offered a way of producing a practical revolver.

On 10 June 1818 Captain Artemus Wheeler of Concord, Massachusetts was granted a patent for a "gun to discharge seven or more times". This was a flintlock revolver carbine

A charge by Mexican lancers at the Battle of Buena Vista during the war with Mexico. Like any war it assisted arms production and development and Colt was quick to profit from it. The Mexican in the centre of the picture has a heavy horse pistol on his saddle bow

which Wheeler hoped to sell to the United States Navy. Only two incomplete specimens exist today, since Wheeler made very little progress with the idea. But he gave a copy of his patent to one Elisha Collier who set forth for England and in November 1818 obtained an English patent for a "firearm combining a single barrel with several chambers to obtain a succession of discharges from one loading". He then set about manufacturing pistols and rifles built according to his patent.

Collier's design differed from that of Wheeler; Collier always acknowledged that Wheeler had the first idea, but insisted that his modifications were of equal value. His pistols and rifles were at first flintlocks, but the design was soon changed to percussion, and many of the earlier weapons were converted. Leaving aside the lock work, which in the percussion models was fairly simple, the most significant feature of the Collier design is that the cylinder was mechanically rotated, controlled by the operation of the trigger and hammer. Two springs bore on the cylinder, one forcing it forward so that the mouth of the chamber closed over the end of the barrel, and the other spring was a torsion spring which attempted to rotate the cylinder. To operate, the cylinder was first loaded in all its six or seven chambers. It was then drawn back, away from the barrel and against the pressure of the spring, until it could be revolved counter-clockwise so as to wind up the torsion spring. Once this was sufficiently wound, the cylinder was eased forward until a chamber engaged with the barrel, which effectively prevented rotation of the cylinder. The pistol was then fired, the hammer igniting the charge in the aligned chamber. As the hammer was drawn back to cock for the next shot, a hook linked to the hammer engaged in a skirt mounted on the rear face of the cylinder and drew the cylinder back, out of engagement with the barrel. As soon as the cylinder was clear, the torsion spring immediately revolved it, and as the next cylinder came into line with the barrel, so a notch in the skirt allowed the hook to disengage and so allow the cylinder to run forward and re-engage with the barrel. As an additional security, the falling hammer rammed a small bolt forward to butt against the rear edge of the cylinder and thus prevent the explosion from blowing it clear of the barrel.

Unfortunately this ingenious system of automatic rotation failed to work quite as well in practice as it did in theory, and although it is known that pistols with this mechanism were made, none survive today, and by about 1824 the torsion spring had been removed from the design. Henceforth the cylinder had to be revolved by hand between each shot, pulling it back to disengage from the barrel, turning it, and then letting it forward to lock the next chamber in place. And although several testimonials as to the accuracy and efficiency of Collier's revolvers have survived, it seems that sales were not sufficient to warrant continued production. By 1828 he had closed down and turned to civil engineering, and he never returned to the gun business.

But as Collier faded from the scene, another name was waiting in the wings, working on his own idea of a revolver pistol. Samuel Colt had been born in Hartford, Connecticut in 1814. At the age of 16 he was a cabin-boy on the sailing ship *Corvo*; according to legend he spent his spare time whittling away at a piece of wood until he perfected a design for a revolver. In truth this story was a later fabrication

of the infant public relations industry. After his tour as a cabin-boy, Colt assumed the name 'Doctor Coult' and travelled around the country fairs of America, turning a dubious penny by intoxicating fairgoers with laughing gas. Whether or not he had ever whittled a wooden pistol is open to question, for he never, as far as is known, received any sort of training as a mechanic, but he certainly had an interest in revolving pistols, and with the proceeds of his medicine show he employed a gunsmith named John Pearson and installed him in a small workshop in Baltimore in 1834. Acting to Colt's instructions Pearson made several working model guns and as soon as he had a satisfactory design, Colt sailed for England to take out English Patent No 6909 of 22 October 1835. He then returned to the United States to take out US Patent 9430X of 25 February 1836. He was just 21.

Colt now obtained some financial backing and opened a factory at Paterson, New Jersey, calling his company the Patent Arms Manufacturing Company. He showed his real vocation here, a vocation for organisation, for advertising, and for understanding and appreciating the principles of modern mass production long before anyone else in the gun trade. His factory was under the supervision of another gunsmith, Pliny Lawton, while Colt busied himself with promoting the products, percussion revolvers, rifles, shotguns and carbines, all using the revolving cylinder principle.

A critical examination of Colt's (or Pearson's) design will show that few of the mechanical features are in any respect original in themselves; the use, for example, of a pawl and ratchet for revolving the cylinder, had been first used in the 17th century. Where Colt scored was in the conjunction of the various features, the general cleanness of the design, and the simple fact that he was astute enough to obtain a patent on the whole lot, a matter which had been neglected by the originators in previous centuries; since no prior claim existed, Colt was able to obtain protection, and having done so he took good care to make it stick.

Colt's first revolver went into production in late 1836 and became known as the 'Texas' model or the 'Paterson' model, from the location of the factory. It was of .34-in calibre, with a $5\frac{1}{2}$-in octagonal barrel and a five-shot cylinder. The nipples were recessed into the back end of the cylinder, which was mounted on a central rod or 'arbor'; the barrel was a separate forging which slid on the arbor, locked into the front of the grip frame ahead of the folding trigger, and was retained by a locking pin which passed through slots in the barrel unit and the arbor. The hammer was cocked by drawing it back with the thumb, an action which at the same time revolved the cylinder by means of a pawl or lever attached to the hammer and which pushed against a ratchet on the rear face of the cylinder. As the hammer went back, so the folding trigger unfolded and sprang out ready to be pressed; there was no trigger guard. The frame was of metal, with wooden butt-grips, and the shape of the butt could be either straight or curved at the buyer's wish. The pistol was generally sold cased, with an outfit of a spare cylinder, bullet and powder flask, cleaning rod, combination tool and cap magazine in separate compartments.

The Paterson model was never intended to be a military pistol but it appears to have found favour among the Texas Rangers. In 1839 Colt had another good idea and patented a built-on loading lever which was fitted beneath the barrel

Peter Newark's Western Americana

PRESENTATION PEARSON-COLT 1835

This unusual piece with its inlaid wooden furniture beneath the barrel has an almost 18th century appearance. It was probably one of the experimental handguns built by Pearson for Colt. The partnership did not last long due to the unreliability of Pearson's work. This weapon has many of the features found in later Colt weapons made at the Paterson factory. The smooth magazine cylinder and folding trigger which did away with the need for a guard. Though this made for a handgun with a pleasingly clean profile its operation could require two hands which was a disadvantage when mounted on horseback

Magazine: 5 shots

Peter Newark's Western Americana

The Colt pistol in the Indian Mutiny; a British officer in a counter-mine waits with his revolver for enemy miners to break through. A musket and pistol are also ready should the enemy prove too numerous for his revolver. The Royal Navy and British Army had acquired a number of Colt weapons and they saw service under conditions as testing as any found in the frontier days of the American West. Colt himself presented handguns to officers as an astute publicity exercise

and which could be used to load and ram the bullet into the cylinder chambers. Prior to this, the Paterson model had to have the cylinder removed for ease of loading; it *was* possible to load it in place on the pistol but it was much simpler to load both the pistol cylinder and the spare cylinder beforehand and then, after firing the first cylinder, reload by simply slipping off the barrel, removing the fired cylinder, replacing it with the loaded spare, replacing the barrel, and continuing. This practice was to continue as long as Colt made percussion pistols, but with the addition of the loading rod it became less common.

Unfortunately though, the world did not appear to be ready for Colt's revolver, and when his financial backer went bankrupt, the company was forced into liquidation, the tools, plant and stock of pistols being sold off for just over $6000 in 1843.

Colt now turned to a totally different project, designing a submarine mine defence system for the US Government and also working on the development of electric telegraph systems. But in 1847 the outbreak of the Mexican War led to a sudden demand for military arms, and General Zachary Taylor, who had been impressed with the quality of the Colt revolvers in the possession of several of his officers, despatched

Captain Sam Walker to see Colt and arrange for the manufacture of a military revolver. Walker made some suggestions as to the form such a weapon should take, Colt produced a design, and in January 1847 he received an order for 1000 pistols.

Colt, of course, had no factory of his own at this time, so he turned to Eli Whitney, a noted gunmaker with a large factory at Whitneyville, Massachusetts and contracted with him for the production of the revolvers. Whitney is frequently called the 'father of mass production' and there is no doubt that he had a fine grasp of the need to standardise parts and split up manufacture so as to attain the sort of volume needed by this type of order. The days of slow and careful hand work by individualist gunsmiths were coming to a close as far as military arms were concerned, and Whitney and Colt were the foremost among those manufacturers who brought this revolution about.

The new model, officially the Model of 1847, more often called the 'Whitneyville Walker' model, was probably the biggest handgun produced in the United States. Of .44-in calibre it was $15\frac{1}{2}$-in long with a nine-inch barrel, had a six-shot cylinder and weighed just over $4\frac{1}{2}$ lb. The whole design was much more robust than the Paterson model, the barrel

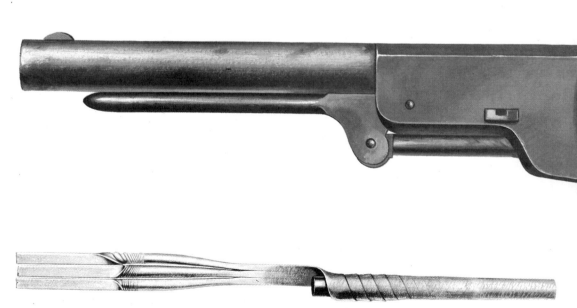

THE WALKER-COLT
.44-in CALIBRE

This pistol, known variously as the Model of 1847, Whitneyville Walker and Walker-Colt is one of the earliest examples of a pistol design that was eventually to become known universally as the Colt. At $15\frac{1}{2}$-in it was one of the largest handguns ever built in the United States and though heavy it was almost indestructible. Despite its bulk it has the long hammer spur and barrel with a comfortable and elegant grip which became readily recognizable Colt features

Weight: 4 lb 9 oz

Magazine: 6 shots

A barrel maker or former with the overlapping bands of steel wrapped around the central core to give the necessary strength

being reinforced at the breech end, a powerful rammer being fitted, and the non-folding trigger protected by a trigger guard. The lock mechanism remained the same, the hammer having to be thumb-cocked before every shot, a system which came to be known as the 'single-action' lock. The system of construction, with the separate barrel anchored in place by a key through the barrel unit and cylinder arbor was also the same.

In November 1847 a second order for 1000 revolvers was received, and from the proceeds of these two orders Colt was able to set up his own factory once more, and in 1848 he moved to Hartford, Connecticut, putting to use much of what he had learned about production in Eli Whitney's factory. He engaged Elisha Root, an excellent engineer, to be his factory superintendent, and in 1848 he began manufacture for commercial sale.

His first model was the 1848 Dragoon, also called the 'Old Model Army' which was very similar to the Whitneyville Walker in general appearance; the principal recognition point is the appearance of a short stub of barrel behind the re-inforced breech piece and in front of the cylinder. This was followed by a smaller model, the .31-in calibre 'Baby Dragoon', with a five-shot cylinder. It appeared with a variety of barrel lengths. In 1849, just as production was getting well under way, the discovery of gold in California set off the famous Gold Rush, and the majority of the prospectors who headed west provided themselves with a Colt revolver, which gave a useful boost to sales and also helped to establish the Colt as the most popular pistol in the West.

In 1851 Colt produced the revolver which is probably the best-known of all his percussion pistols, the 'Old Model Navy' in .36-in calibre. It followed the same lines as the earlier models but was rather more graceful, had an octagonal barrel 7½-in long, and a six-shot cylinder. As was common with all Colt designs of that period, the circumference of the cylinder was engraved with a martial scene; previous models had depicted battles with Indians and a stage-coach ambush, but the 1851 pistol cylinder showed a naval battle between the Texas navy and the Mexican navy which had taken place in 1845, and it is this, and not any official adoption, which led to the pistol being called the 'Navy' model.

Colt, was, in fact, in an enviable position in the United States, since his Patent 9430X was a 'master patent'. It specifically protected the mechanical method of revolving the cylinder and of bolting the cylinder to the frame so as to hold it securely locked in alignment with the barrel during

COLT PATERSON
.34-in CALIBRE

This pistol patented in 1836 was Colt's first design. Made at the Paterson factory in New Jersey it had a 9-in barrel and folding trigger. The trigger fell forward when the hammer was thumbed back and was ready for firing. When the shooting was over it could be flicked back to be held in position by a retaining catch. Though Colt did not design these weapons for a military market they did prove popular with men like the Texas Rangers. There were few original features in early Colt weapons, but he was astute enough to patent his pistols as entire designs, unlike earlier gunsmiths who were content to register individual parts like locks or magazine feeds

Magazine: 5 shots

Federal and Confederate forces clash during the American Civil War. The war was a stimulus to gunmakers in the North and South and made the fortunes of men like Colt

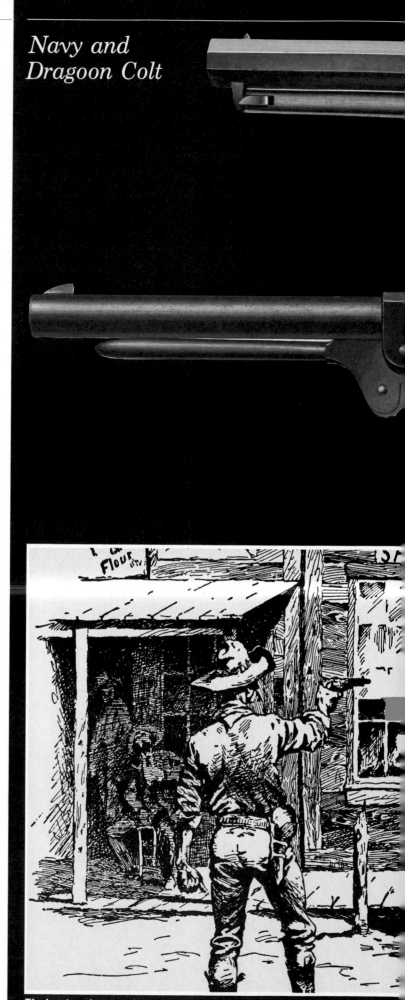

Navy and Dragoon Colt

firing. The specification was so broadly drawn that Colt was able to stifle any competition which appeared, since he was able to show that his patent covered *any* method of mechanically revolving and locking a cylinder. As a result, he enjoyed a practical monopoly until the patent expired in 1857.

It will be recalled that Colt had also taken out an English patent at the same time (1835); he never took steps to put this patent to use by manufacturing in Britain, and since the period of protection at that time was restricted to 14 years, it expired in 1849. In 1851 Colt went to England to exhibit his revolvers (and shoulder arms using the revolving principle) at the Great Exhibition, and he aroused considerable interest there. This interest was increased by some well-thought-out publicity stunts, such as withdrawing a number of revolvers from his exhibit and selling them to officers of the 12th Lancers, then under orders for South Africa, and, after the exhibition closed, presenting the entire collection to various people and organisations who might possibly be useful to him in the future. His aim behind all this was to bring the Colt revolver to the favourable notice of the British Army and Navy, an aim which had some success in 1854 when some 9500 Model 1851 'Navy' revolvers were bought by the Royal Navy. In 1853 production of revolvers began in a London factory, in Pimlico, and it was from this source that the Navy contract was filled.

But Colt was not alone in the military revolver field in Britain, even though he still enjoyed his near-monopoly in the United States. In 1851 Robert Adams, a partner in the gunsmithing firm of Deane, Adams and Deane, produced a revolver which was to become highly competitive with the Colt design and which, indeed, was a far better weapon.

The most significant feature of the Adams design was that it was a 'solid-frame' revolver, and thus inherently stronger than the 'open frame' design of the Colt. Solid frame construction meant that the barrel, frame and butt were all forged from one solid piece of metal, an opening being cut into the frame to allow the cylinder to be inserted. Thus the barrel was rigidly attached to the frame by both the normal attachment beneath the barrel and by a 'top strap' which passed across the top of the cylinder to the 'standing breech', that portion of the frame immediately behind the cylinder in which the hammer operated. The cylinder revolved around an arbor, or axis-pin, which could be withdrawn from the front of the frame by releasing a spring latch; removing the arbor allowed the cylinder to be taken from the frame for cleaning or reloading.

The lock mechanism was totally different to that of Colt. It was of the 'self-cocking' type, in which it was not necessary to thumb back the hammer and then pull the trigger. All that was needed with the Adams revolver was to pull the trigger; this first raised the hammer, revolved the cylinder to the next chamber, locked the cylinder in place and then released the hammer, all in one swift movement. This lock system was not new, but Adams refined it considerably and made it into a practical and smooth-working system which found considerable approval amongst army officers whose prime criterion was a pistol's performance in close combat. But when, in the early 1850s, the British Army and Navy went looking for pistols, they used the more formal yardsticks of accuracy and long range to reach a decision, and in these respects the Colt

The handgun in use to bring an argument to a permanent end between a cowbo

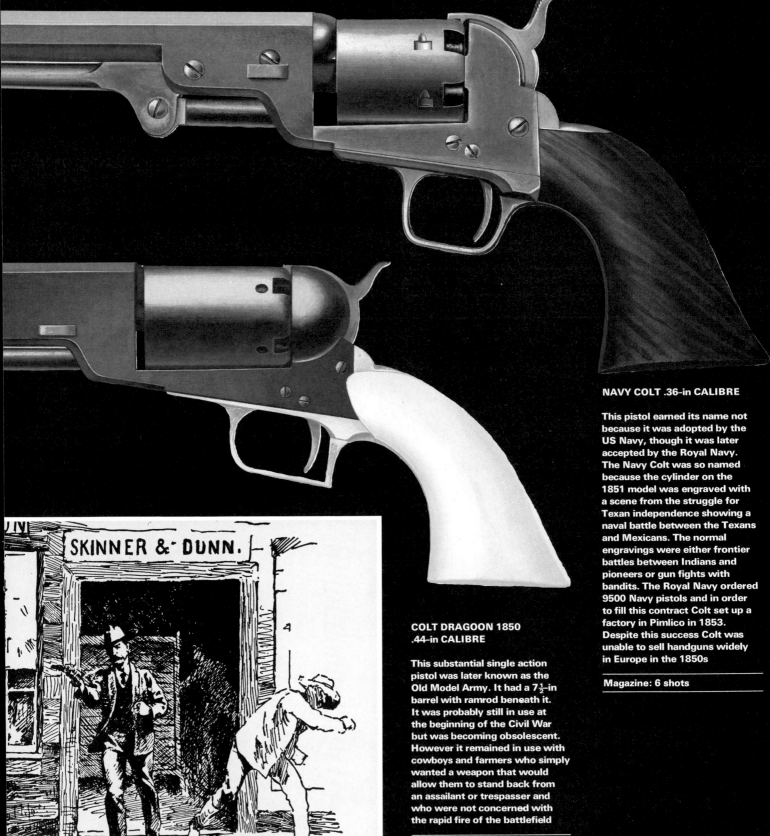

NAVY COLT .36-in CALIBRE

This pistol earned its name not because it was adopted by the US Navy, though it was later accepted by the Royal Navy. The Navy Colt was so named because the cylinder on the 1851 model was engraved with a scene from the struggle for Texan independence showing a naval battle between the Texans and Mexicans. The normal engravings were either frontier battles between Indians and pioneers or gun fights with bandits. The Royal Navy ordered 9500 Navy pistols and in order to fill this contract Colt set up a factory in Pimlico in 1853. Despite this success Colt was unable to sell handguns widely in Europe in the 1850s

Magazine: 6 shots

COLT DRAGOON 1850 .44-in CALIBRE

This substantial single action pistol was later known as the Old Model Army. It had a $7\frac{1}{2}$-in barrel with ramrod beneath it. It was probably still in use at the beginning of the Civil War but was becoming obsolescent. However it remained in use with cowboys and farmers who simply wanted a weapon that would allow them to stand back from an assailant or trespasser and who were not concerned with the rapid fire of the battlefield

Magazine: 6 shots

SKINNER & DUNN.

nd the citizen of a frontier cowtown

Peter Newark's Western Americana

1851 was slightly superior to the Adams, which led to Colt obtaining the orders. Service use, however, soon showed that the self-cocking feature of the Adams and its heavy .44-in calibre proved superior in the ultimate test of real warfare to the single-action and .36-in calibre of the Colt, and after seeing the results of both weapons in the Crimean War and in practical use in India, the Army changed its mind and, in 1855, decided on the Adams revolver as the standard weapon. For those people who preferred the more deliberate single-action system of the Colt revolver lock, Adams altered his system in 1855 so that it could be used either way; the hammer could be thumbed back and then deliberately released by the trigger for more accurate firing, or it could be simply fired by trigger pressure in the self-cocking mode when speed was needed. Since this system gives the advantage of both systems, it has since come to be universally known as the 'double-action' lock and eventually became the general standard pattern on revolvers.

It seems probable that it was the lack of thumb-cocking which had caused Adams' revolver to be resisted for so long by the British Army, and the invention of the double-action Frederick E B Beaumont lock was actually due to a Lieutenant

Beaumont of the Royal Engineers who, using the Adams self-cocking lock as his basis, patented a double-action lock in February 1855. He then assigned this patent to Adams and went into partnership with him, and the subsequent Adams revolvers are more correctly known as the 'Beaumont-Adams'. The Board of Ordnance ordered 100 revolvers for test in the following month, and, after the success of these tests, ordered 2000 revolvers later in the year.

Adams and Beaumont-Adams revolvers were also produced under licence by a number of makers, notably Francotte of Liège in Belgium and the Massachusetts Arms Company in the United States, although the latter had to wait for the expiry of the Colt patent before they could begin to sell the Adams design in America. Colt was less given to licensing, but one notable exception to this was his issue of a five-year licence to the Königlich und Kaiserlich Maschinenfabrik of Innsbruck, in Austria in 1849. This well-equipped factory began by making exact copies of the 1848 Dragoon model, the only difference between them and the genuine Colt being the inscription 'KK Masch Fab Innsbruck' on the right side of the frame and 'Patent 1849' on the left. However the Dragoon was a little too much of a good thing for the

ALLEN AND THURBER PEPPERBOX .34-in CALIBRE

Patented in 1845 by Ethan Allen this handy pocket pistol had a double action. It was one of the more common pepperbox weapons in the days of '49 when the gold rush fever attracted ruthless men to the United States. Though .34-in was a low calibre by the standards of the time, the pepperbox was not intended to drop a horse or rider at 100 yards, but to give a man a chance to back out of a saloon, shooting

---

Magazine: 6 shots

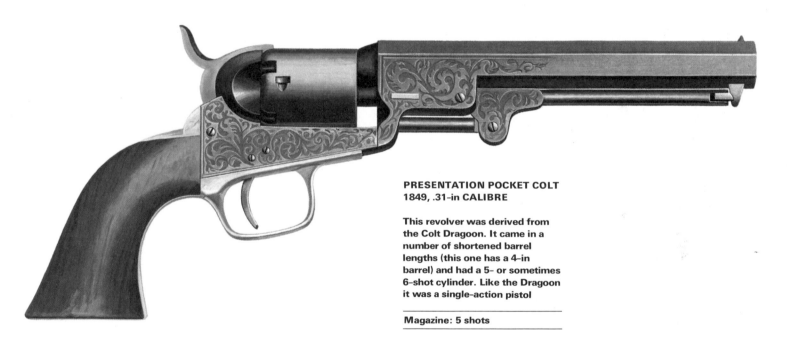

PRESENTATION POCKET COLT 1849, .31-in CALIBRE

This revolver was derived from the Colt Dragoon. It came in a number of shortened barrel lengths (this one has a 4-in barrel) and had a 5- or sometimes 6-shot cylinder. Like the Dragoon it was a single-action pistol

---

Magazine: 5 shots

European military to stomach, and after some complaints, the Innsbruck concern redesigned the pistol, reducing its size and weight until it became almost identical with the 1851 Navy revolver. The calibre of the Innsbruck model was 9.5-mm, with a 135-mm barrel and a six-shot cylinder, and numbers were purchased for evaluation by the Austrian Navy. But no major order was forthcoming and when the five year licence expired, the Innsbruck factory gave up the production of Colt copies and turned to other things.

While Colt and Adams were the best-known names of the period, largely due to their excellent publicity sense, there were several other revolver makers pressing their products on the public, and some of these managed to prosper.

One defect of early revolvers was that the interface between the front of the cylinder and the rear of the barrel was a sizeable gap, due largely to the lack of precision in manufacturing methods of the time. Some of the energy of the cartridge's explosion was wasted by leakage at this gap, as the bullet went up the barrel, and, what was a good deal worse, there was always the danger that flash from this gap could spread across to the other chambers and, if the bullet was not close-fitting, could ignite the charges therein and

discharge the lot – the same sort of problem that had dogged the turret revolver. At least in the cylinder revolver the chambers were all pointing away from the person who held it.

It will be recalled that the Collier revolver allowed the cylinder to ride forward in its arbor so as to positively engage the chamber mouth with the rear of the barrel. This was intended simply to give a positive alignment between the chamber and the barrel, but in about 1853 Witton & Daw, London gunmakers, produced a revolver which in general outline was based on the Colt open-frame but which incorporated a to-and-fro motion of the cylinder. In this case it was specifically claimed as a method of obviating the leakage of gas around the joint, and the dangerous consequences attendant thereon, and it appears to have found some favour. As well as adding to safety, it undoubtedly added to the accuracy and velocity of the bullet by curing the leakage of gas and ensuring that the bullet passed into the barrel without any misalignment. Such misalignment was usually overcome by the sheer force of the bullet movement, but it usually caused some perceptible amount of lead to be shaved from one side of the bullet as it entered the barrel, to the subsequent detriment of balance and accuracy.

INVENTORS AND PATENTS

In 1852 the laws regarding the obtaining of patents in Britain were brought up to date and considerably improved. One of the improvements was to reduce the cost and also to provide protection throughout the United Kingdom instead of requiring the inventor to take out separate patents in England and Wales, Scotland, Ireland, and the Channel Islands. This had involved a cost of £393 to obtain complete protection, but the new Act of 1852 reduced the cost to £25 for the whole of the UK. However, it also introduced the principle of automatically voiding the patent after the third or seventh year unless renewal fees were paid, though the full term of protection remained at 14 years. As a result more inventors were encouraged to take out patents; if, within three years, they were unable to interest a manufacturer they could allow the patent to lapse, avoiding further expense. If, on the other hand, they found the idea had some profitable application, then the renewal fees would be paid and full protection continued. It might be noted that there was no leeway in this ruling; in more than one case a patent lapsed at the end of the three-year or seven-year period even though the patentee appeared with the necessary renewal fee within two or three days. On the due date the axe fell, and no amount of subsequent representation could alter the fact that the patent was now void. This feature is of some importance in the subsequent history of pistols, as will be seen.

Because of the lesser cost of patent protection, more patentees appeared after 1852 and many of them were concerned with revolver and pistol applications. One such was James Webley of Birmingham who, together with his brother Philip, took out several patents in 1853 to cover various detailed aspects of revolver design. Philip appears not to have had much interest in revolvers, but James managed to manufacture a well-designed, if not particularly robust, revolver from about 1854 onwards. These models are usually known as the 'Webley Longspur' pistols, from the exaggerated spur to the hammer which allowed thumb-cocking of the single action lock without having to shift the grip on the pistol. They were open-frame revolvers which used a similar crossbolt to Colt's in order to secure the barrel unit to the cylinder arbor; the larger 'Holster' and 'Belt' models were five-chambered, while the small 'Pocket' model was six-chambered. Calibres were, in the parlance of the day, 48-gauge, 60-gauge and 120-gauge, which equates to .459-in, .426-in and .338-in calibres.

Although Webley became a contractor to the Board of Ordnance for various items of gun furniture, he never managed to interest the Board in his revolvers, probably because they were firmly convinced of the superiority of the solid-frame, double-acting Beaumont-Adams pistol, but he managed to make a reasonable living out of selling his revolvers on the commercial market, though due to his system of hand-manufacture and finishing, he could never compete with the low-priced mass-production products of Adams or Colt.

James Webley died suddenly on 28 March 1856; on the following day his patent covering the 'Longspur' revolver fell void owing to failure to renew the licence fee – an oversight quite understandable in the circumstances but which was incapable of rectification. The business was carried on under the name of James Webley, since doubtless there was considerable goodwill in the name, but there is little doubt that it was being run by Philip Webley who, later in the year, began to include the words 'Pistols and Revolvers' in his trade advertisements. For some years the business continued, largely producing revolvers for sale to small gunsmiths who then engraved their own names on them, only the inscription 'Webley's Patent' indicating their true origin.

Another 1853 patentee was William Tranter, another Birmingham gunmaker and one of high repute. His principal patents were related to various types of lock mechanisms, and the revolvers he produced were solid-frame designs (this feature being licensed from Robert Adams) with peculiar double triggers. One trigger sat, in the usual way, within the trigger guard, while the other passed through the guard and was exposed below it. Pulling back on the lower trigger cocked the hammer; pulling the upper trigger fired the pistol. This arrangement gave the advantages of the single action lock in respect of light trigger pull and steady aim, but also gave the speed advantage of the double-action lock. In 1856, however, Tranter had second thoughts and produced a conventional double-action lock with a single trigger. This, he hoped, would compete with the Beaumont-Adams for military recognition, but in this he was unsuccessful. Numbers of double-trigger and single-trigger revolvers to Tranter's patents were made in Belgium and the US, under licence.

Also in 1856 the partnership of Deane, Adams and Deane was dissolved, and one of the partners, John Deane, set up as Deane and Son in London. In 1858 William Harding patented a totally new design of revolver, and Deane allied himself with Harding to produce the 'Deane-Harding Patent Revolver'. The unique feature was the construction of the frame. We have seen that Colt adopted the open frame in which the barrel unit was held to the cylinder arbor by a cross-bolt, while Adams took the opposite choice and perfected a completely solid frame. Tranter had, in fact, patented a third system which involved a solid frame as far as the front of the cylinder, after which the barrel was made separately and screwed into the frame, but he did not use this form in his revolvers; this was simply due to the fact that he was providing Adams with most of his solid frames and it was easier and cheaper for him to licence this idea from Adams and stamp out the frames on the same machinery. But Harding now devised a system of producing what amounted to a solid frame revolver but which was really in two pieces. The butt unit had its frame carried forward beneath the cylinder where it ended in a notch with a cross-piece. The standing breech, in front of the hammer, terminated in a lug with a hole in it. The barrel unit had a top strap which ended in a double lug with holes through, while the section beneath the barrel ended in a hook. To assemble the revolver the cylinder was slipped on to its arbor, and then the lower hook on the barrel section was engaged with the cross-pin at the lower front of the frame. The whole barrel unit was then hinged back until the double lugs fell at each side of the single lug on the standing breech, whereupon a pin was thrust in to lock the whole thing together.

Other features of Harding's design included a lever-rammer beneath the barrel, and a double-action lock. Calibres were 54-bore (.442-in) for the 'Army' model and 120-bore (.338-in) for the pocket model. However, although the pistol appears to have been licensed to other makers, as well as

TRANTER 30-BORE DOUBLE-TRIGGER REVOLVER

Patented in 1853 by William Tranter a Birmingham gunmaker this revolver has a double trigger. The lower trigger which passes through the guard cocked the hammer, pressure on the second fired the pistol. The advantages of this system was that it needed only a light pressure on the trigger which made for more accurate shooting. However unlike single-action weapons there was no need to thumb back the hammer and so shooting was quicker

Magazine: 6 shots

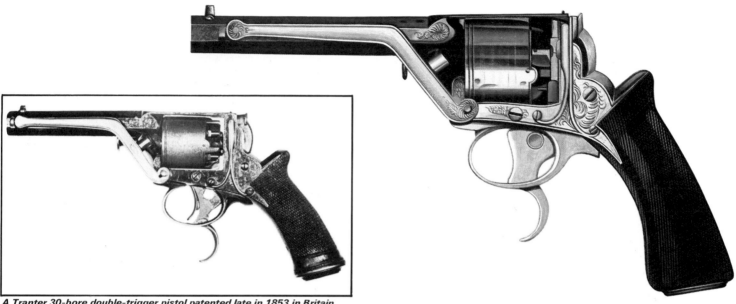

A Tranter 30-bore double-trigger pistol patented late in 1853 in Britain

G Boothroyd

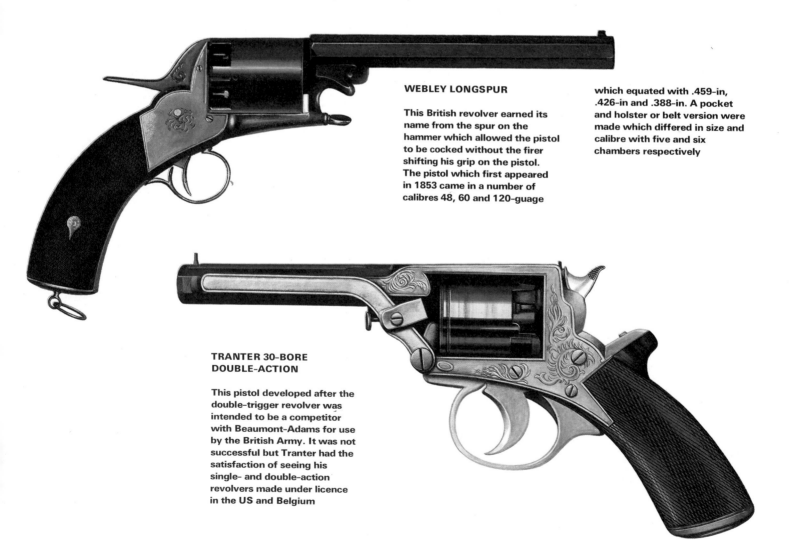

WEBLEY LONGSPUR

This British revolver earned its name from the spur on the hammer which allowed the pistol to be cocked without the firer shifting his grip on the pistol. The pistol which first appeared in 1853 came in a number of calibres 48, 60 and 120-guage which equated with .459-in, .426-in and .388-in. A pocket and holster or belt version were made which differed in size and calibre with five and six chambers respectively

TRANTER 30-BORE DOUBLE-ACTION

This pistol developed after the double-trigger revolver was intended to be a competitor with Beaumont-Adams for use by the British Army. It was not successful but Tranter had the satisfaction of seeing his single- and double-action revolvers made under licence in the US and Belgium

COLT ROOT WORKING MODEL 1855

This unusual .265-in working model was made from Charter Oak wood by Eli K Root. Root was Colt's factory superintendant and persuaded Colt to adopt the side hammer. This was cheaper and later became popular with carbines. The Root design also featured a solid frame and a separate barrel which screwed into the frame

Magazine: 6 shots

A scout with the US Cavalry saves a pioneer and her daughter from a grisly fate. The pistol was a useful back-up for the Winchester carbine and though still underpowered by modern standards its heavy round was a good man-stopper since the soft lead expanded when it hit

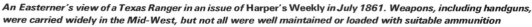
An Easterner's view of a Texas Ranger in an issue of Harper's Weekly in July 1861. Weapons, including handguns, were carried widely in the Mid-West, but not all were well maintained or loaded with suitable ammunition

Peter Newark's Western Americana

Peter Newark's Western Americana

being turned out by Deane, it does not seem to have prospered and production apparently died out in the early 1860s.

It is not without interest, in view of the description of frame designs given above, to note that Colt produced a solid frame pistol in 1857. This weapon was designed by Elisha Root, Colt's factory superintendent, and featured a solid frame with the barrel screwed in (as in Tranter's patent) and with an unusual side-mounted hammer, from which feature it is usually called the 'Root Side-Hammer Model', though its official factory name was the 'New Model Pocket Pistol'. Another new feature was the adoption of the 'sheath trigger' or 'stud trigger' in place of the usual type of trigger. The frame was formed into a protruding sheath in place of the usual trigger guard, and the trigger was completely concealed within this sheath until the hammer was cocked. Thus it could be carried in the pocket without fear of the trigger catching in the act of withdrawing the pistol. As the hammer was thumbed back (it was, of course, a single-action lock) the trigger was drawn clear of the sheath in a position to be pressed. A small lever rammer fitted beneath the barrel, in usual Colt style and, although these were not marketed until 1897, they are invariably marked 'Colt's Patent 1855' on the barrel.

1857 also saw the expiry of Colt's master patent, and a number of other manufacturers had been perfecting designs and waiting for the chance to use them. Many were little more than out-and-out copies of Colt's basic layout, but there were some which were completely original. Unfortunately, originality in pistol design is no guarantee of success; indeed, it can often be just the opposite, and few of these designs prospered. Nevertheless, they are worth recording as examples of yet another way of reaching the same conclusions as had Colt, Adams and Tranter.

The Pettingill revolver, for example, was probably the first 'hammerless' design to appear in the United States, a design which was to achieve much more prominence in later years. It was a solid-frame revolver with octagonal barrel and a Colt-inspired lever rammer, but the rear portion of the frame completely concealed the hammer mechanism. It was a double-action (obviously, since there was no hammer to be cocked) with a highly-modified hammer which moved directly forward to strike the cap mounted at the rear end of each chamber. In .44-in calibre, two models, the 'Army' and 'Navy' were produced, but few were made and they are extremely rare today.

The 'gas-seal' idea – that of moving the cylinder forward so as to make a tight seal with the barrel – reappeared in the Savage-North revolver of 1856. The solid frame was of bronze, with an under-barrel lever-rammer, and the chambers had nipples mounted at right-angles to their axis, so that the chamber lined up with the barrel had its nipple pointing upwards. The hammer struck downwards and was controlled by an oddly-shaped actuating lever surrounding the trigger. This lever was in the form of a figure eight, the upper aperture being the space for the normal trigger and the lower aperture a finger-rest by which the lever could be operated. The firer placed his second finger into this lower aperture and pulled the lever back; this cocked the hammer, withdrew the cylinder from contact with the barrel and revolved it to the next chamber. The firer then pushed the lever forward which left the hammer cocked, forced the chamber into

SAVAGE-NORTH PERCUSSION REVOLVER .36-in CALIBRE

This unusual design which was patented 17 June 1856 had a 7¾-in octagon rifled barrel. The figure-of-eight trigger and lever cocks the hammer and operates the cylinder. When a new round is in position the cylinder moves forward to engage in the mouth of the breech as the lever is returned to the forward position. This produces an almost gas-tight joint and improves the performance of the pistol

Weight: 3 lb 7 oz	
Magazine: 6 shots	

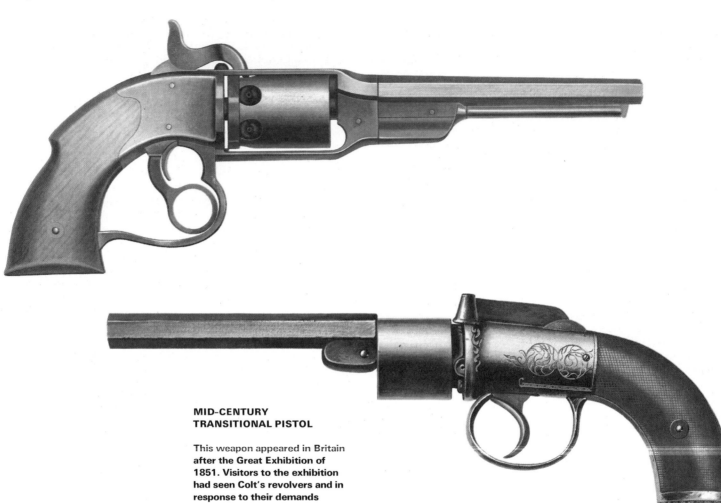

MID-CENTURY TRANSITIONAL PISTOL

This weapon appeared in Britain after the Great Exhibition of 1851. Visitors to the exhibition had seen Colt's revolvers and in response to their demands gunsmiths had produced a weapon which was derived from the pepperbox. Most were 55-bore or .38-in with a 6-in barrel. They had a double action

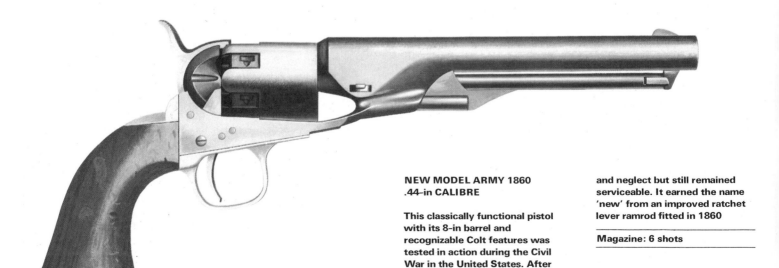

NEW MODEL ARMY 1860 .44-in CALIBRE

This classically functional pistol with its 8-in barrel and recognizable Colt features was tested in action during the Civil War in the United States. After the war it passed into the hands of farmers, cow hands and bandits where it received abuse and neglect but still remained serviceable. It earned the name 'new' from an improved ratchet lever ramrod fitted in 1860

Magazine: 6 shots	

contact with the barrel and locked it. He then pressed the trigger in the usual way to cause the hammer to drop on to the cap. The pistol was designed by H S North and made by the E Savage company of Middletown, Connecticut. It was calibre .36-in and six-chambered, and at least three models were made from 1856 to the middle 1860s.

The Remington Company of Ilion, New York had been in the arms business for many years, largely concerned with military contract work and the supply of finished barrels to gunsmiths, but in 1858 they entered the revolver field with a six-shot weapon to the patents of Frank Beals. These were solid-frame weapons with removable cylinders to facilitate loading, and the principal novelty of Beals' design was that the cylinder was revolved by an outside-mounted pawl on the left side of the frame above the trigger. Although this was prone to derangement, it seems to have answered well enough and large numbers of these pistols, in .44-in and .36-in calibre, were sold. A pocket model in .31-in calibre was also popular.

One of the most remarkable weapons of the period and, strangely, one which prospered, was the 'Le Mat Grapeshot Revolver'. Jean Alexandre François Le Mat was born in France and later went to the United States where he practised as a physician. How he came to dream up his pistol design is not known, but while living in New Orleans in 1856 he took out his first patents. He later returned to France and, in conjunction with Charles F Girard of Paris, began manufacture. The significant feature of Le Mat's design was the presence of a second barrel beneath the usual barrel, charged with a loading of small shot. The basic revolver was an open-frame model with nine-shot cylinder of about .40-in calibre, while the shot barrel was commonly an 18- or 20-bore. The shot barrel acted as an arbor for the cylinder and was provided with a special vent and nipple, to which a movable hammer head could be diverted by pressing a switch. In the normal course of events the hammer fell on the caps of the cylinder chambers, but in extremis the switch was pressed and the opposition blasted by the shot charge.

While Le Mat was away in France arranging for the production of his revolver, events in the United States began to move towards the Civil War, which, of course, precipitated manufacture of firearms in massive quantities. Much of the manufacturing capacity of the United States was in the North, which put the Union in a favoured position, but even so the production had to be stepped up to keep up with demand and Union agents were soon off to Europe to purchase weapons there. The standard issue revolvers of the Union forces were of Colt design, the Army Model 1860 and the Navy Model 1861, both of Colt's usual open-frame type. The Army model was a six-shot of .44-in calibre, while the Navy model was a six-shot of .36-in calibre.

In the Southern Confederacy, pistol factories sprang up overnight, their products being virtual copies of Colt designs. One such model was the Leech and Rigdon .36-in calibre; Charles H Rigdon had begun making swords in Memphis, fled from there to Columbus, Missouri, in the face of a Union advance, and finally settled in Greensboro, Georgia, in 1863 where he produced the revolvers. Similar models were produced under the names of 'Griswold and Greer', 'Spiller and Burr' and the 'Columbus Firearms Mfg Company'. Doctor Le Mat now organised the supply of Le Mat revolvers

to the Confederacy; many were made in France, about 1000 are said to have been made in Birmingham, and it is believed that a small quantity were made in the Confederacy. In spite of their appearance in some numbers, it seems that they were less highly regarded than the Colt or the Colt copies.

The American Civil War is a milestone in firearm development in that it saw the end of the muzzle-loading percussion era of firearms and the beginning of the breech-loading cartridge-fired era, and we must now turn to consider the steps which had been made in the matter of convenience in loading.

Although the Colt, Adams and other contemporary revolvers were muzzle loaders, it should not be automatically assumed that loading them was the same business of shaking loose powder and a lead ball that had been the standard in the days of the matchlock; there had been some improvements. As early as the latter part of the 16th century it had become normal to prepare a complete charge and a bullet and wrap them in a paper package for convenience in reloading. The complete package became known as a cartridge, and the technique of loading was to tear off the end of the paper cartridge, usually with the teeth, and shake the powder into the pistol barrel, reserving a small quantity for priming the pan. The remains of the paper were then wadded up and rammed down on top of the powder so as to confine it, and finally the ball was likewise rammed down. In order to make the ball a tight fit it was frequently rammed down over a small fragment of paper or cloth known as a 'patch'.

This system continued until about 1850, when the growing popularity of revolvers led to several inventors taking a closer look at the cartridge to see whether the loading process could not be simplified. At much the same time the elongated, conical bullet came into favour, and this lent itself to the manufacture of self-contained cartridges. The general result was to have a thin paper tube containing the propelling charge and tied to the end of the bullet. Thus the complete unit could be dropped into the chamber of a revolver and seated with one quick stroke of the rammer. Seating also deformed the tapered cartridge and ruptured it so as to allow an easy passage for the flash from the percussion cap.

The idea was reasonable, but it tended to give rise to fouling in the chambers and in the middle 1850s the combustible cartridge came along, one in which the paper was treated with nitric and sulphuric acids so as to turn it into a variety of nitro-cellulose, sufficiently inflammable to be completely consumed when the charge was fired and leave no dangerously smouldering residue in the chamber. Another variation was the 'skin' cartridge, actually made from a seamless piece of animal intestine; this could be made much thinner than paper, giving an equally good chance of being totally consumed as the combustible cartridge but without the problems of manufacture. All these cartridges were inserted into outer paper tubes, usually with a ribbon or thread to allow them to be removed before loading; this outer tube was merely protection against damp and damage during storage and handling. During the Civil War William Montgomery Storm, a well-known American gun designer, came up with the idea of treating skin cartridges with a gutta-percha varnish, which effectively turned them into combustible cartridges without the problems attendant upon the nitration process.

PERCIVAL AND SMITH MAGAZINE PISTOL 1850, .32-in CALIBRE

Invented by Orville Percival of Moodus, Connecticut around 1840 this ingenius piece was 14½-in long. However he did not register the patent until 9 July 1850 in the name of Percival and Smith who manufactured the arm. The front chamber contained 40 .32-in calibre balls while the rear held the proper amount of powder and tube with fulminate pellets. To load, the chambers were swung upward in a half circle which dropped the fulminate, powder and ball into position in the barrel. The sleeve holding the chambers sealed the charge when the magazines were returned to their original position. A firing pin on the hammer exploded the fulminate pellet and this detonated the powder charge

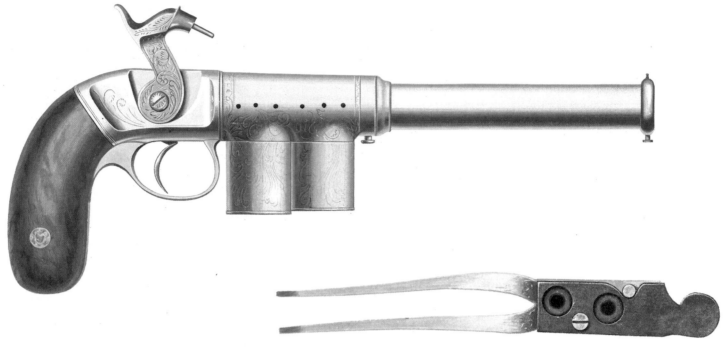

BULLET MOULD, JOHN ADAMS 1866

Accessories for civilian firearms included bullet moulds, since all the gun owner needed was a supply of lead to make his own bullets. The copper or chrome jacketed round with its own cartridge case was developed in the 20th century when accuracy and muzzle velocities increased. The lead slugs were in practice particularly lethal since they were inclined to distort if they hit bones and being slow moving would lodge in their victims

Cartridge loading of this sort had one extremely useful by-product; it forced gunsmiths to standardize on a few popular calibres instead of making whatever they thought convenient and providing the buyer with a bullet mould. As we have seen, calibre was still spoken of in 'gauges' or 'bores'; the figure being the number of lead balls of the bore diameter which went to make up one pound in weight. This accounts for the odd-sounding calibres which were settled on in the early days; the Colt .36, for example, was 100-bore, while the .44 was 54-bore and the .31 150-bore. As long as the owner of a gun had to cast his own bullets, the bore was of little consequence provided he was provided with a mould of the correct size when he bought the gun. But when prepared cartridges began to be made by companies who specialised in ammunition and were not in the firearms business, then it made sense for the makers of pistols to settle on some few standard dimensions. As we shall see, there has never been a shortage of gun designers ready to produce pistols of odd calibre together with special cartridges to suit, in the hopes that their pistol would be such a roaring success that they could make their fortune from the subsequent ammunition sales, but this aim has rarely been achieved.

The first example of a self-contained cartridge which could be loaded into a weapon from the breech end, was that developed by Samuel Pauly, a Swiss engineer employed in the French arsenal at St Etienne in 1812, and his design incorporated all the basic features which have been perpetuated in cartridges ever since. The cartridge had a paper body rolled around the front end of a rimmed base which was turned from metal or wood. A central recess in the base carried a small charge of detonating powder, protected from damp and retained in place by a slip of varnished paper. Beneath this pellet was a hole passing through the base to the interior of the paper tube, in which lay the charge of black powder. The bullet was placed on top of the charge and the paper tube was then gathered over the top of the bullet and tied with thread. Pauly also produced a simple single shot pistol with drop-down barrel, so that the barrel could be unlatched and swung clear of the standing breech, the cartridge inserted into the chamber and the barrel closed and latched. A hammer then struck a firing pin which, in turn, struck the detonating composition and fired the cartridge.

Pauly made slight modifications in subsequent years, such as specifying a ductile metal for the base-piece in order that it would accommodate itself to the breech more easily. In 1813 his cartridge and guns (rifles and pistols) were tested by order of Napoleon but nothing came of this; opinions vary as to whether this was due to Napoleon's lack of vision or, more probably, to the expense of equipping an army with the system. One drawback was that each cartridge base had to be lathe-turned by hand, a time-consuming business which could hardly have provided the vast quantities needed for Napoleon's armies. For civilian owners the problem was less demanding, since they bought the gun with a dozen or so prepared cartridges and then had to sit down, after firing these off, and roll their own paper tubes and make up their own cartridges from the base-pieces. Such a procedure may have been acceptable to civilians but not soldiers.

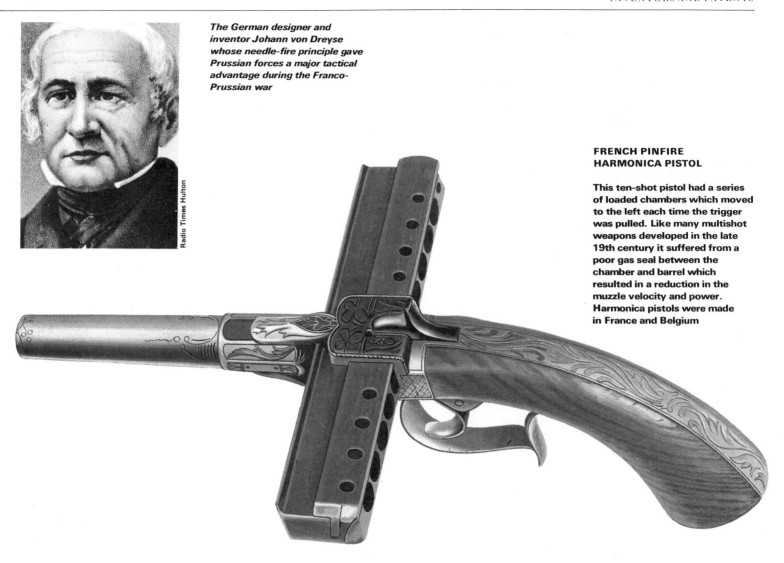

The German designer and inventor Johann von Dreyse whose needle-fire principle gave Prussian forces a major tactical advantage during the Franco-Prussian war

Radio Times Hulton

FRENCH PINFIRE HARMONICA PISTOL

This ten-shot pistol had a series of loaded chambers which moved to the left each time the trigger was pulled. Like many multishot weapons developed in the late 19th century it suffered from a poor gas seal between the chamber and barrel which resulted in a reduction in the muzzle velocity and power. Harmonica pistols were made in France and Belgium

One of Pauly's employees was a Prussian named Johann Nikolaus von Dreyse. In 1814 von Dreyse left Paully and returned to Sommerda, in Prussia, to receive his certificate as a master gunmaker and to take over the running of his father's workshop on the latter's death. He made a number of rifles, which appear to have been influenced by what he had learned from Pauly, but these were not successful and he turned to manufacturing hardware items and then percussion caps. In about 1826 he developed his 'needle-fire' gun, which introduced the turn-bolt system of breech closing, and with this he also introduced a novel cartridge. The von Dreyse cartridge was a cylinder of paper with a flat base, at the forward end of which sat a bullet supported in a papier-mache 'sabot'. In the bottom of the sabot was a small pill of detonating powder; below this, filling up the remainder of the cartridge, was the propelling charge. Thus the ignition unit was in the centre of the cartridge. Firing was performed by a long needle (from which came the name of the gun) which, when the trigger was pressed, was forced through the base of the cartridge to strike the detonating composition and crush it, igniting the powder.

It will be realised that the principal weak link in von Dreyse's system was that the rear of the chamber had to be effectively sealed by the breech mechanism, since there was no form of sealing in the cartridge. It took von Dreyse some time to solve this satisfactorily, which he eventually did by making a coned face to the bolt which mated with a suitable coned seat in the mouth of the chamber, and as a result it was

not until 1841 that the rifle was accepted for use by the Prussian Army. In 1850 he introduced a revolver using the same principle of operation; this was a solid frame weapon with the body oddly extended behind the cylinder in order to accommodate the bolt and needle. On pulling the trigger the bolt was thrust forward to close the rear of the chamber and the needle then passed through to fire the cartridge. On releasing the trigger the bolt and needle were retracted.

In the eyes of some inventors the drawback of the von Dreyse and Pauly cartridges was the paper tube, which was easily damaged and prone to distortion from the weight of the bullet in the end. The appearance of conical bullets suggested one way out of this problem, and in 1840 Joseph Cooper patented an elongated bullet with a cavity in the base which contained a charge of detonating powder; there seems to be no record of Cooper taking the idea any further or making a gun to suit, but in 1847 an American, Walter Hunt, patented an improved idea in which the cavity was enlarged to take a propelling charge of powder and closed by a perforated metal cap. Ignition was done by the usual type of percussion cap on a nipple at the rear of the chamber, the flash from which passed through the vent and through the hole in the closing cap to fire the charge. Hunt built a rifle to suit this cartridge, and the design was later improved to become the Jennings rifle of 1850. Shortly after this two partners, Horace Smith and Daniel Baird Wesson, improved the Hunt idea by placing a small detonating cap in the base of the bullet, and thus produced a completely self-contained cartridge.

An officer gives the order to withdraw to a screen of troops as Indians charge towards a makeshift stockade. Indian fighting needed quick reactions, steady nerves and above all a reliable weapon. The handguns that lasted in the West were among the best in the world

The Volcanic magazine feed

Smith and Wesson produced both rifles and pistols to take their cartridge, from about 1852 onwards; in 1854 the patents were taken over by a company formed for the purpose and the weapons were renamed the 'Volcanic'. Smith and Wesson appear to have been well aware of the defects of the design and they got out in 1856 and set about forming their own pistol company. The Volcanic company went bankrupt in 1857 and were bought out by one of the original stockholders, a man named Winchester, a haberdasher who knew nothing about firearms but was a shrewd businessman. But he wasn't shrewd enough to make much of a success out of the Volcanic, and he eventually hired a brilliant mechanic called Tyler Henry to take the Volcanic idea, give it a thorough shaking, and produce the lever-action rifle with which Winchester's name has always since been associated. But that is another story.

The volcanic pistol, which concerns us here, is probably the earliest of a class more generally called the 'mechanical repeater', and as such it was about thirty years ahead of its time. Beneath the barrel of the pistol was a tubular magazine into which a number of the self-contained Volcanic cartridges could be loaded. The trigger guard was actually a lever, hinged at the front and shaped into a ring at the rear end, a ring into which the firer fitted his second finger. On thrusting the lever forward a breech block was drawn back and a 'lifter' lifted a cartridge from the rear end of the tubular magazine to the open chamber. At the same time the rearward stroke of the breech block pushed the hammer back and cocked it. When the lever was pulled back, the breech block was thrust forward, driving the cartridge into the breech and locking the block by a simple arrangement of levers. The lifter went down again and a spring thrust a fresh cartridge on to it. On pulling the trigger the hammer fell and struck a firing pin passing through the breech block, which in turn struck the detonating cap at the rear end of the cartridge to explode the charge and thus drive the bullet out of the barrel.

While the Volcanic principle was quite sound, its execution left a good deal to be desired. Misfires were common, and since there was no proper sealing arrangement at the rear of the breech other than the face of the breech block butting against the rear of the chamber, the gas leakage was considerable and the bullet consequently lacked velocity and power. Compared to the contemporary Colt it was unreliable and inaccurate, and in a country where pistols were expected to work for their living, that was enough to damn the Volcanic. In spite of some inspired publicity work by Oliver Winchester, after he took over the company, the Volcanic rifles and pistols went out of production before 1860.

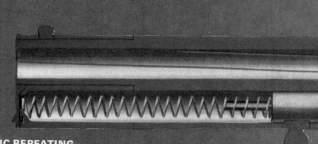

VOLCANIC REPEATING PISTOL 1854

Using the Smith and Wesson cartridge the Volcanic pistol had a tubular magazine beneath the barrel. The operation of the lever allowed a round to come back and by a further movement of the lever it was pushed up into the breech. The firer then squeezed the trigger which depressed the sear and allowed the hammer to come forward and strike the firing pin. Though it was an advanced design there was trouble with the ammunition and the company eventually went out of production

'When Horseflesh Comes High' a painting by the artist Charles M Russell. Rustlers are returning the fire of a posse that has surprised them running off horses. The rustler on the ground is armed with a Winchester carbine a weapon using the Volcanic magazine principle. The rounds are enclosed in a tubular magazine beneath the barrel

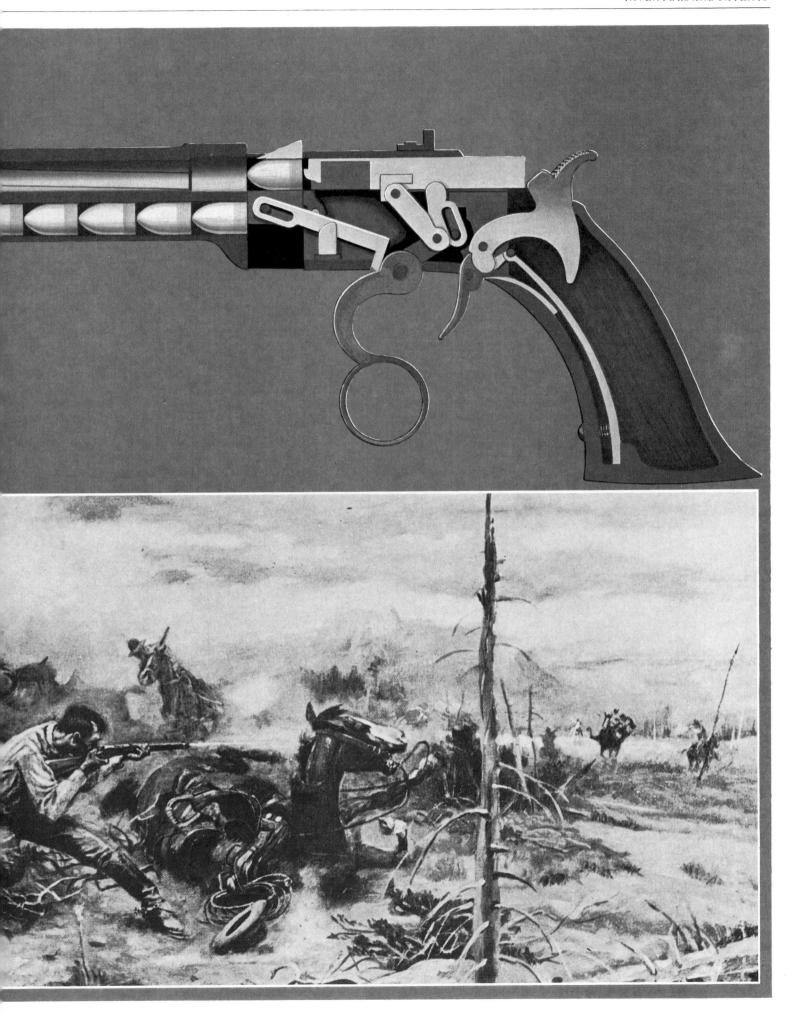

CARTRIDGE AND PINFIRE

A far more practical device had appeared in Europe when Bernard Houllier, a Frenchman, devised a thin metallic case containing the propelling charge and with the detonating cap contained within the base. A short metal pin passed through the side of the cartridge base to rest on the cap. When loaded, this protruded through a slot in the edge of the chamber so that it could be struck by the falling hammer. The pin then fired the cap and the cap ignited the charge. Moreover the thin metal case, during the explosion, momentarily expanded to seal the rear end of the chamber against the escape of gas but, when the pressure died down, was sufficiently elastic to contract again so as to allow the case to be withdrawn from the chamber. This was the 'Pin-Fire' cartridge, and it was the first self-contained cartridge to become an unqualified success. Its use was widely expanded by another Frenchman, Eugene Lefaucheaux, to such a degree that he is often credited with having invented it, and as a practising gunsmith Lefaucheaux produced a large number of designs for rifles, shotguns and pistols to take the pinfire cartridge.

The pinfire revolver, as popularised on the continent, employed a cylinder with the chambers bored through the full length and with slots at the rear of each chamber. The hammer was designed to fall vertically on to the exposed pin in the topmost chamber. Apart from these changes, the revolvers were either open-frame or solid-frame types already pioneered by Colt and Adams, and there was little mechanical novelty about them. But at the time – the 1850s – pistol manufacture was slowly turning from the hand-work system to the use of machinery to allow great quantities to be turned out cheaply, and thus the pinfire revolver, from its ease of operation and its cheapness of manufacture, soon became the commonest arm in Europe.

The same Houllier who patented the pinfire in 1846 also patented another form of self-contained cartridge. In effect, he took the existing percussion cap, formed a rim in the closed end and put a bullet in the open end. The detonating mixture was held within the hollow rim, and the firing arrangement of the proposed weapon· was to trap the rim between the edge of the gun chamber and the falling hammer, so deforming the rim and firing the compound inside. As with the pinfire, Houllier seems to have been content to patent the idea and leave it for somebody else to put into practical form. In the case of the 'rimfire' cartridge, it was taken up by another French gunsmith, Louis Flobert, who applied the idea to a series of single-shot pistols and rifles in small calibres, which, from their low power and small noise, were soon popular for indoor shooting.

It will be recalled that Smith and Wesson left the Volcanic company in order to pursue their own ideas in 1856. One of the things which prompted them to do this was the rimfire cartridge. They were far from satisfied with the self-contained Volcanic cartridge and in 1854 they obtained a patent for an elongated form of the rimfire Flobert cartridge into the case of which they had added a small charge of black powder. This, of course, improved the power and velocity and took it out of the 'salon rifle' class. In 1851 Daniel Wesson's brother had been involved in a lengthy and bitter lawsuit over alleged infringement of one of Colt's patents, and with this example to guide them, Smith and Wesson took a good look at the existing patents to see if there was any impediment to their

Top: A pinfire cartridge, the pin struck the small blob of mercury fulminate to detonate the powder. The round was therefore very unstable since each one had its own firing pin
Middle: The rimfire cartridge had a band of fulminate around the rim and was therefore safe and simple to make. Rimfire ammunition is still in use today for small calibres like .22-in
Bottom: A Colt cartridge, the powder and slug come in a packet with the percussion caps separate. Though this is a safer round to carry compared to the pinfire it takes longer to load

EUGENE LEFAUCHEAUX PINFIRE REVOLVER

This weapon produced in 1860 in 7-mm was widely copied in Europe despite a patent registered in 1854. It was the earliest breech loading revolver to be commercially available. It is an interesting pistol which falls between the percussion types developed in the United States and the later centre fire cartridge types

Magazine: 20 shots

LE MAT PERCUSSION REVOLVER 1856 .40-in CALIBRE

This French revolver offered its owner the option of firing single .40-in rounds at his target or, should the target come too close, of blasting it with a 20-guage shotgun round. The shotgun barrel was beneath the .40-in calibre barrel. Though this might be an excellent sales pitch it presented the owner with the ammunition resupply problem of carrying 20-guage cartridges as well as a stock of .40-in rounds

Magazine: 9 shots

A 20-shot revolver by Henrion Dassy and Heuschen of Liege Belgium

Colt pistols bring an argument over a card game to an abrupt end. Many pistols were poorly maintained by cowhands and shooting standards were not high. This man however is the winner of the gunfight and perhaps the card game too

STARR PERCUSSION REVOLVER 1856, .44-in CALIBRE

This heavy revolver was made by Starr Arms Company of Yonkers, New York. The company produced handguns between 1856–67 in .44-in and .36-in calibre. Their double-action weapons found wide use in the Civil War, but demand fell off with the cessation of the war and the glut of surplus weapons. Both the North and the South set up arms factories during the war and small gunsmiths found their skills at a premium particularly in the less industrialized South

Magazine: 6 shots

producing a revolver to take the rimfire cartridge. In the process of this search they discovered that an ex-employee of Colt named Rollin White, an indefatigable inventor and patentee, had taken out a patent (US Pat 12648 of 3 April 1855) which included, among many other claims, the principle of "extending the chambers through the rear of the cylinder for the purpose of loading them at the breech from behind". White had apparently offered this patent to Colt, who had refused it, a singularly short-sighted act since the wording of the claim was such that here was another 'Master Patent' which could successfully prevent anyone else from boring chambers through a cylinder from end to end. Smith and Wesson appreciated this point and bought the patent from White on terms which were highly advantageous to them; they paid White a royalty on every revolver produced, but left White the responsibility (and expense) of fighting potential infringers in the law courts. As a result, much of White's profit from the royalties was swallowed up by legal expenses as he fought off innumerable attempts to copy the idea. Doubtless jaundiced by this experience, he appears to have left the firearms business entirely in later years, to eventually make his fame and a modest fortune by inventing the White Steam Car.

With the Rollin White patent firmly in their possession, Smith and Wesson went into production with their 'Number One' revolver in 1857, and maintained their monopoly for the full 14 years life of the patent. While the rimfire cartridge was successfully applied to rifles and long arms in general during this period, the revolver application was securely in the hands of Smith and Wesson and they made the most of it. No breech-loading revolver was made in America between

Slocum sliding-sleeve revolver patented in April 1863

G Boothroyd

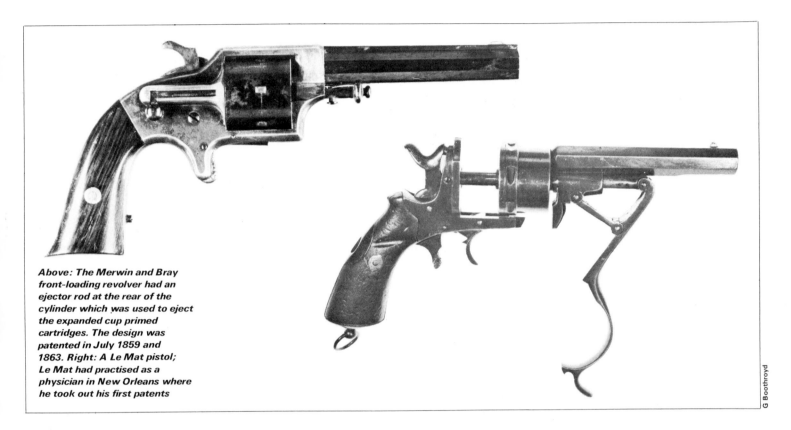

Above: The Merwin and Bray front-loading revolver had an ejector rod at the rear of the cylinder which was used to eject the expanded cup primed cartridges. The design was patented in July 1859 and 1863. Right: A Le Mat pistol; Le Mat had practised as a physician in New Orleans where he took out his first patents

G Boothroyd

1856 and 1869 without either paying royalties to Smith and Wesson or losing their production to them.

The Smith and Wesson revolver was a five-shot weapon with a new type of frame construction, generally called the 'tip-up' revolver. The barrel unit was hinged to the frame at the front end of the top strap, and locked to the bottom front of the frame by a simple catch. The cylinder revolved on a simple arbor, and by releasing the catch and tipping up the barrel, the cylinder could be removed for loading and re-loading, the empty cases being punched out of each chamber by means of the rod which protruded beneath the barrel. The calibre was .22-in, the cartridge being perpetuated to this day as the '.22 Short', and it attained immediate popularity; it is recorded that by 1864 Smith and Wesson were two years behind on their orders and were contracting with other companies to make pistols to their design. Unfortunately, the development of the rimfire cartridge was difficult, and making heavier calibres led to problems with the rims blowing out; because of this it was some time before a .32-in calibre version appeared, and since these weapons were deficient in 'stopping power' they were of little use as combat revolvers during the American Civil War. It is this reason which accounts for the continuation of the percussion revolvers in large calibres for many years after the introduction of the breech-loading cartridge weapon. Nevertheless, the principle had been proved; from now on it was simply a matter of gradual improvement of the principle until the percussion weapon and time consuming and awkward muzzle-loading were completely swept away.

In spite of Smith and Wesson's grip on the bored-through cylinder, there were still a number of ingenious inventors who thought that they could find a way around the patent, and a number of remarkable designs appeared in the USA over the next few years. In order to achieve their aim it was necessary to develop some new form of cartridge as well, since the rimfire could only be used with a breech-loader. Typical of these was the Merwin and Bray 'Front-loader', a revolver with a solid frame which greatly resembled the contemporary Smith and Wesson except that the chambers in the cylinder were not bored entirely through. Instead, they ended in a solid rear wall pierced by a small hole which allowed the firing pin, on the hammer, to enter the chamber when the trigger was pressed. The cartridge which went with this arm was a metal cylinder carrying a cap at the rear and a bullet in the front, with the front edge of the cylinder belled out so as to grip the walls of the chamber by friction. These cartridges were thrust into the chambers from the front end; on firing, the firing pin passed into the chamber and struck the cap in the more-or-less normal way. To eject the empty cases a rod ejector lay alongside the pistol frame, behind the cylinder, and was thrust forward to pass through the firing pin hole and push the case out to the front. Patented in 1859, the Merwin and Bray was an ingenious idea and was one of the few practical designs which evaded the Smith and Wesson net.

Less practical was the Slocum 'Sliding Sleeve' revolver of 1863. In this, the cylinder was a grooved carrier into which steel sleeves, loaded with rimfire cartridges, could be slipped. A solid shield at the rear of the cylinder was bored with the necessary hole for the firing pin. In effect, it was almost a bored-through cylinder, and it could use normal ammunition, but the multi-part construction evaded the strict letter of the patent, so Slocum survived; though his pistols seem not to have sold in great numbers.

A variation of the Merwin and Bray front-loaded was the famous Moore 'Teat-fire' pistol, another front-loading revolver which like the Merwin design, used an all-enveloping cartridge with the mouth belled out around the bullet so as to hold it in the chamber. Where Moore differed, and where he achieved fame, was in forming the cartridge into a rounded base end with a small teat which contained the fulminate priming composition. The rear of the chamber was solid but had a tiny hole bored through it, and through this hole passed the teat, positioned so that it would be struck by the falling hammer when the pistol was fired. Moore seems to have had some success with this design; certainly the pistols are not uncommon today and the peculiar cartridge is to be found in most ammunition collections.

Less well-received was the 'Crispin' revolver which split the cylinder into two halves, the front half being attached to the tip-down barrel and the rear half permanently attached to the frame. The rear half had blind holes, while the front section had holes bored all through, so that when the barrel was hinged up and locked in place, the effect was a cylinder with the rear ends of the chambers completely closed. At the junction line, each chamber had a sloping hole, which aligned with a slanting firing pin inside the revolver's top strap. Finally, the cartridge was a tapering brass case with a bullet in the front end, and, around its waist, a raised rib which contained the fulminate priming. To work the pistol it was broken open for loading and the cartridges inserted, base first, into the rear end of the cylinder. The barrel was then hinged up so that the front section of the cylinder enveloped the bullets. The rib around the cartridge case sat in a groove at the cylinder joint line. When the hammer was released, it struck the firing pin which then passed through the oblique cut in the chamber to strike the raised rib and thus fire the fulminate inside. It was an involved way of going about things, and it did not prosper; only one or two specimens of the Crispin revolver remain and no specimens of the peculiar cartridge are known to exist.

Another way to get around the troublesome patent was, of course, to use a weapon which didn't need a cylinder. The Remington company were particularly ingenious in this respect and they produced two weapons which were moderately successful. The first went down in history as the 'Zig Zag Derringer', since it was a short, pocket pistol similar to the single-shots made by Henry Deringer, but it used a revolving principle operated by zig-zag grooving. Instead of a cylinder, the Remington design had a cluster of six barrels which all rotated; while the front section was grooved and fluted to save weight and improve appearance, the rear of the cluster was a plain cylinder with a zig-zag groove incised into the surface. Inside the pistol frame, a pin, connected to the trigger, moved in the groove and, due to the zig-zag form, rotated the whole barrel cluster when the trigger was pulled. After a short distance of the trigger stroke the barrel cluster was locked and the internal striker driven forward to fire the rimfire .22-in cartridge. Since the whole barrel cluster revolved, it could hardly be classed as a 'bored-through cylinder' within the terms of the Rollin White patent. Remington's other design was the 'Remington-Rider' pistol, so-called from being due to the patents of William H Rider. This was a

magazine pistol using a tubular magazine underneath the barrel. A hinged breech block could be drawn back and opened by a spur above the frame, resembling the hammer spur of a revolver; behind this was the hammer, with a slightly lower spur, and opening the breech automatically cocked the hammer. Opening the breech also operated a lifter which raised a cartridge from the magazine; releasing the breech block allowed it to run forward and chamber the cartridge, and also sent the lifter down again for another round. When the trigger was pressed, the hammer went forward, its firing pin passing through a hole in the breech block to fire the cartridge; as the hammer came up behind the breech block, it acted as a support to prevent the explosion of the cartridge forcing it open. In order to accommodate five shots in the magazine of such a short pistol, and also so as to keep the operating stroke of the breech short, a special 'Extra Short .32 Rimfire' cartridge had to be developed for this pistol. It appears to have been moderately popular, some 15000 being made between 1871 and 1888.

These pistols were, however, relatively weak; and Remington, realising that a heavy revolver was a more marketable proposition in those days, came to terms with Smith and Wesson over the matter of the White patent, so that they were able to produce revolvers with bored-through cylinders. In this way their 'New Model .44' percussion revolver had its chambers bored out and suitable modifications made so that it accepted a .46-in rimfire cartridge, one of the largest-calibre rimfire rounds ever used in a pistol.

Strangely, although the rimfire cartridge became immensely popular in America, it made relatively little impression in Europe at that time. Most of the cheap revolvers appearing in Belgium were chambered for the various pinfire cartridges, and this appears to have taken the place of the rimfire in that country. Elsewhere the designers were attempting to make progress with the central fire cartridge, and since the Rollin White patent had no validity in Europe, there was no artificial restraint on them. In the USA, few designers were interested in improving pistol ammunition until such time as they would be free to make a suitable weapon, and the technique of making rimfire ammunition had made such steps that rifle ammunition was also largely rimfire. But the rimfire was not well suited to high velocity loadings; and, things being what they were, European designers always had one eye cocked towards military applications, where high pressures and velocities were the order of the day.

The development of the centre-fire cartridge is not a tidy and simple story; it is a long and involved saga of tiny modifications by various men over a long period of time which eventually emerged as the centre-fire cartridge as we know it today; a drawn brass case with a primer inserted into the centre of the base and one or more flash holes passing through into the body of the case so as to ignite the contents when the cap is struck.

One consequence of the arrival of the metallic cartridge was that inventors began to give some thought to the problem of getting the cartridges in and out of the pistol in a convenient fashion. The Smith and Wesson and the early European revolvers adopted a simple method; the firer removed the cylinder completely, either by breaking open the revolver frame – as with the Smith and Wesson 'Tip-up'

MOORE TIT-CARTRIDGE REVOLVER .30-in CALIBRE

This brass nickel-plated weapon with an engraved frame bears the patent 'Moore's Pat Fire Arms Company Brooklyn NY' and around the rear of the cylinder 'D Williamson's Patent January 5, 1864'. The rear of the cylinder is solid except for a small circular opening through which the 'tit' of the cartridge slips. It rests on a circular boss which acts as an anvil when the hammer descends. In the front of the cylinder on the right side is a small loading gate

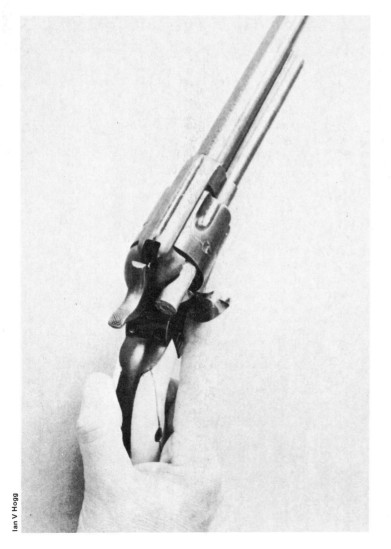

Above: A French service revolver of 1892 showing the Abadie modification. The cylinder gate is on the right and when swung down against spring pressure an internal cam pushes the hammer strut to the rear which allows the trigger to operate the cylinder rotation without cocking the hammer. The photograph shows the cam behind the cylinder pawl and in front of the hammer strut.
Left: A single-action .45-in Colt Frontier revolver showing the gate open to receive a round

Ian V Hogg

G Boothroyd

A Thornton .45 revolver; this patent submitted by 'Baron Thornton' was for a lock designed by Jean Warnant. Thornton swindled Warnant, but this did not deter the British who adapted the lock for their Enfield service revolver of 1880

Ian V Hogg

– or by simply removing the arbor pin around which the cylinder turned, so that the cylinder was free to drop out of the frame. Once out, the empty cylinder could be loaded with cartridges and replaced in the frame. Having fired off the cartridges, the cylinder was once again removed and the empty cases were punched out of their chambers, one by one. The Smith and Wesson carried a heavy pin beneath the barrel for this purpose, while the European makers preferred to utilise the cylinder arbor pin for the task. It was a slow system, and it soon became common practise to carry a spare cylinder, fully loaded, which could be dropped into the frame to replace the empty one and thus allow fire to be continued.

The first improvement on this system was the adoption of 'gate loading', which is generally held to have been invented by a Belgian gunsmith named Abadie. If he did so, then he either drew a poor patent or failed to patent the idea at all, since within a few years it was in use by almost every gunmaker and it is still in use today. In this system a section of the standing breech behind the cylinder – usually on the right-hand side of the frame – was either cut away or arranged to hinge to the side, so exposing the rear end of one chamber. The pistol hammer was provided with a 'half-cock' notch, so that it could be pulled back part-way and thus withdraw the cylinder locking bolt and allow the cylinder to be turned freely by hand. Cartridges could now be inserted through the 'gate', into the exposed chamber, the cylinder being turned round as each chamber was loaded until the cylinder was full. Then the gate was closed and the hammer drawn back to full cock position, ready to fire.

To get the empty cases out, Abadie fitted an extracting rod on to a hinged arm, pivoted in front of the pistol frame below the cylinder arbor. The extracting rod lay within the hollow arbor when not in use. When required to eject the empty cases, the gate was opened and the ejecting rod pulled forward to remove it from the arbor, then swung sideways on its hinged arm until it was lined up with the cylinder chamber and gate, and then thrust back so as to force the case out through the open gate. Again, the process had to be repeated for every chamber, turning the cylinder by hand between each one. Once empty, the rod was returned to its place within the arbor and the chambers could then be reloaded.

As several people found, there was one slight drawback with this system; occasionally the hammer would slip from the half-cock position and, falling, would fire the cartridge in the chamber beneath the hammer while the process of reloading was going on. This was extremely dangerous, and Abadie solved it by linking the gate with the hammer mechanism, so that when the gate was opened a shaped cam on its lower end would firmly press the hammer back and disconnect the hammer from the trigger. Thus any inadvertent pressure on the trigger could not accidentally fire the pistol, nor could the hammer slip free of its half-cock notch. Cumbersome as the gate-loading system was, it had the advantage of simplicity; it was easy to operate, there was nothing to go wrong, and it was cheap and simple to make. As a result, it prospered for many years on the cheaper kinds of revolver, and it was perpetuated in the heavy 'Frontier' types based on Colt's design.

However, even its staunchest supporters had to admit that it was slow and fiddly and was a definite drawback when a revolver was used in a life-or-death affair and speed of reloading became a vital question; although as one critic observed, if you hadn't hit the other fellow in six shots, you were in trouble anyway. But for military use, where enemies were coming by the dozen, rapid reloading had its advantages. Extraction of the spent cases was the slowest part of the proceedings, and in an endeavour to speed things up a number of inventors tried to perfect methods of automatically ejecting the spent cases while the revolver was being fired. Most of them relied on a simple lever arm across the top of the standing breech, with a claw on the end which engaged behind the rim of the cartridge case in the 'one o'clock' position of the cylinder. As the hammer fell, so the inner end of the arm was struck by the hammer's top face, thus causing the claw end to fly out and so eject the empty case. The first successful attempt at this seems to have been that of the Austrian inventor Sederl in 1880, and a number of revolvers to his design were made by the German gunsmith Berbard Bader.

More common is the similar British design patented by Silver and Fletcher in 1884. But the nearest this idea came to military adoption was in the Swiss Schmidt revolver of 1882; Schmidt incorporated an extractor patented by Krauser into some of the prototypes of this revolver, but the Swiss Army turned the idea down fairly quickly. Like so many firearms inventions, these automatic ejectors worked very nicely in the workshop or showroom, but they tended to be a good deal less perfect out in the field, which was where it counted.

They relied implicitly on two things; firstly that the weapon and ammunition were spotlessly clean and properly lubricated and secondly that the cartridge case was always of the same ductility and always required the same amount of effort to remove it from the chamber. Once dirt entered the chamber, or the hinge of the ejector arm became dry, or a cartridge of slightly soft brass was used which expanded tightly into the chamber when it was fired, then not only did the ejector fail to work but it also reduced the effective blow of the hammer and was highly likely to cause the revolver to misfire, so making things even worse. Silver and Fletcher attempted to overcome this by arranging their extractor to be placed out of action while the revolver was being fired, then brought into operation so that the trigger could be rapidly pulled half-a-dozen times to clear the cylinder without prejudice to firing. Even so, the idea failed to catch on.

POWER IN THE HAND

The year 1869 was a watershed in the history of the handgun. That was the year that the Rollin White patent on bored-through chambers in revolver cylinders, owned by the Smith & Wesson Company and used by them to obtain a virtual monopoly of revolver manufacture in the United States, ended and the floodgates were opened. Scores of gunsmiths began producing thinly-disguised copies of the original Smith & Wesson rimfire revolvers to meet public demand. Many of these were extremely cheap and of poor material; they had no refinements of extraction, had single-action locks which meant that the hammer had to be thumbed back for every shot, and their triggers were plain studs of metal concealed within a sheath on the frame until the action was cocked. Retailing for a dollar or two, principally in .22, .32 and .38 rimfire calibres, they well deserve the title they later acquired Suicide Specials, fitted for nothing more accurate than short-range self-destruction. Nevertheless, they sold by the tens of thousands and still turn up today; and still work.

However they can hardly be considered to be in the main stream of pistol development, and parallel with these trade offerings, some of the better class of manufacturer began to look to the prospect of giving Smith & Wesson a hard time. The Colt Company, though, were slow to make technical advances. Their first reaction was to do nothing more involved than produce replacement cylinders for their old percussion revolvers, together with new hammers, so that the pistols could be returned to the factory and converted to use modern ammunition in place of powder and ball. Then in 1871 they produced their .44 Open Top Rimfire model, which was little more than the old open-frame percussion design completely reorganised for metallic cartridges – practically a newly made conversion. It failed to prosper and for a very good reason.

In 1870 Smith & Wesson, not resting on their laurels, had produced their .44 American model, one of the immortals. It was a hinged-frame model using the automatic ejecting system patented by Dodge and King in which a central star plate automatically moved away from the cylinder as the barrel was swung down, forcing the empty cases out of the chambers. Because of the immense gain in leverage with the long barrel, no jammed cartridge could resist this method of extraction, and the .44 American was soon selling as rapidly as it could be built, such fastidious practitioners as Wyatt Earp, Jesse James and General Custer being among the customers. Against such opposition, there was little hope of Colt gaining much ground with their Open Top model. But the tides of fortune were soon to change.

Shortly after the introduction of the .44 American, the Russian Army decided it needed a modern revolver to arm cavalry and artillery troops, and they despatched a mission to America. According to legend, the Grand Duke heading the mission went hunting with Buffalo Bill Cody and was impressed by Cody's .44 American revolver. He was rather less impressed with the accuracy, which fell short of Continental military standards; this was due to the poorly-fitting bullet. The technical members of the mission redesigned the whole cartridge, opening out the case slightly and making the bullet slightly fatter and heavier so that it was a tighter fit in the barrel and carried better. It gave a 100 ft/sec improvement in muzzle velocity and vastly improved the accuracy. The Russians then asked for some small changes in the pistol: the addition of a spur on the grip so that the pistol did not slip

Samuel Colt, founder of one of the world's great firearms companies

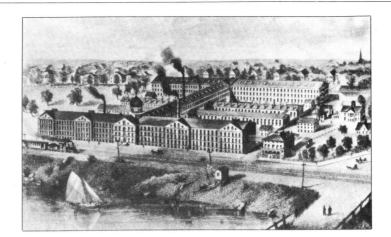

The Colt factory depicted in a print of 1860

SMITH & WESSON .44 RUSSIAN

Between 1870 and 1878 about 215,000 of these pistols were made for the Tsar's army and they were also sold commercially. It was the first successful heavy-calibre hinged-frame revolver and was also made under licence by Löwe of Berlin for many years.

Normally with a 6½ inch barrel, other lengths can also be found

Weight:	2 lb 8 oz
Muzzle velocity:	770 fps
Cylinder:	6 shots

SMITH & WESSON .44 NO. 3 SINGLE ACTION

This model is basically a development of the .44 Russian model; the grip is slightly different and the finger-rest under the trigger guard is omitted. It fired the same .44 Russian cartridge, and became extremely popular in the USA both as a self-defence gun and as a target revolver. Models in .45 Webley, .32-44, .38-44, .44-40 and .38-40 were also made, the smaller calibres principally as target pistols since they gave less recoil than the powerful .44 Russian cartridge

Weight:	2 lb 8 oz
Muzzle velocity:	770 fps
Cylinder:	6 shots

through the hand when recoiling, a finger-rest beneath the trigger-guard, and a barrel length of $6\frac{1}{2}$ in. With all this agreed, they then gave Smith & Wesson a contract for 215,704 pistols, a task which took the company five years to execute, turning out 175 pistols a day. It was a manufacturer's dream come true; nothing to do for five years but produce pistols and bank the money.

Smith & Wesson were so busy that they had little spare capacity to satisfy the domestic market, and in this, Colt saw their opportunity. If they could produce a sound and reliable heavy pistol, particularly one which would satisfy the US Army, they could virtually take over the market in the US, and this they proceeded to do. And the pistol with which they did it was another of the immortals, the Model 1873, or 'Frontier' or 'Peacemaker' as it is variously known.

Technically, the Frontier model wasn't a patch on the .44 Russian; it was a solid-frame revolver, single-action, with gate loading and rod ejection. The ejector rod tended to bend far too easily in use; the cylinder arbor pin had a habit of loosening during firing and suddenly jarring out; and the mechanism of the trigger and lock was notoriously prone to break. But it sold in its thousands and men swore by it. The principal reason for their enthusiasm was that no matter what happened, it was always possible to fire the Colt one way or another. If the trigger spring broke, you could thumb back the hammer and let it slip; or you could slap the hammer back with the free hand, the practice known as 'fanning'. If the ejector broke, you could pull out the cylinder pin and poke the empty cases out. If the mainspring broke, you could bang the hammer with a rock to make it fire. As a weapon for use in the rougher and more remote corners of the world, it was without equal, and, added to all that, the proportions were such that it pointed instinctively and was the perfect weapon for snap shooting at fleeting targets. Finally, like all good designs, it looked right; it had that indefinable correctness of line and proportion that instantly distinguishes good from bad.

As a result, the Model 1873 stayed in production until 1941, when Colt found better things to occupy their time and machinery. After the war the demand for Colt Frontier models was greater than ever, and several manufacturers produced copies. At last Colt themselves responded to the clamour and went back into production in 1955. The model is still in production today. Although generally thought of as a .45 pistol, it has been turned out in almost every conceivable calibre from .22 rimfire to .476 Eley.

The Model 1873 gained its first success by being adopted by the US Army, and some 36,000 were delivered between 1873 and 1891, all in .45 calibre and all with $7\frac{1}{2}$ in barrels. At the same time civilian production went ahead, the plainly finished .45 selling for only $15, another factor in its success. 357,859 were made before production stopped in 1941.

In Europe, at this time, other famous names were looking at revolvers. The Rollin White patent had not been effective there, but the development of handguns had not been particularly fast. There was no Wild West Frontier in Europe which demanded handguns by the thousand, and much of the production was of small-calibre pocket pistols. But the Franco-Prussian War started military minds to work, and in the last quarter of the 19th century, armies were being re-equipped with some modern weapons. With fat military contracts in the offing, revolver design suddenly became worth while.

COLT .45 PEACEMAKER

Properly known as the Single Action Army, 1873 this revolver has become part of history. It was in continuous production from 1873 to 1941, and then after a pause began again in 1955 to continue to the present day. Barrel lengths from 3 to $7\frac{1}{2}$ inches have been made, and it has been produced in almost every calibre from .22 to .476. The basic design was so strong that no change was necessary in order to allow the firing of modern high-velocity loads such as the .357 Magnum

Weight: 2 lb 4 oz

Muzzle velocity: 870 fps

Cylinder: 6 shots

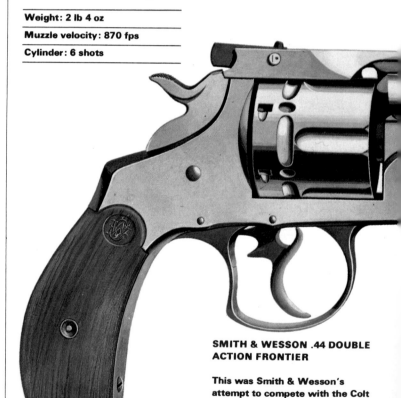

SMITH & WESSON .44 DOUBLE ACTION FRONTIER

This was Smith & Wesson's attempt to compete with the Colt Frontier model, and it was one of their few failures. It was derived from the .44 Russian but had a longer cylinder so as to take the .44-40 Winchester Centre Fire carbine cartridge, and was fitted with a double-action lock. Slightly over two thousand were sold in the late 1880s

Weight: 2 lb 6 oz

Muzzle velocity: 975 fps

Cylinder: 6 shots

By 1900 the Wild West was not quite so wild and the gunslingers had long since gone to Boot Hill, but these Texas rangers of the 1890s with their Colt Peacemakers and Winchester rifles kept the old traditions alive

Western Americana

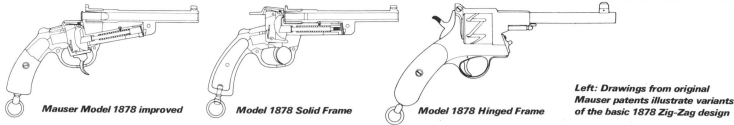

Mauser Model 1878 improved   **Model 1878 Solid Frame**   **Model 1878 Hinged Frame**

Left: Drawings from original Mauser patents illustrate variants of the basic 1878 Zig-Zag design

Peter Paul Mauser had made his name with the Prussian Army's rifle, and he was to go on in that field until Mauser became synonymous with military rifles in later years. But in the 1870s he decided to try to get a military revolver adopted as well. The resulting weapon has gone down in history as the Mauser Zig-Zag because of the novel form of operation. It was a hinged-frame, tip-up, revolver, and the cylinder's outer surface was incised with a zig-zag groove around its circumference. This groove engaged with a pin in the lower part of the frame, which, in turn, was moved by the operation of the trigger. As the trigger was pulled, or the hammer drawn

back, to cock the pistol, the pin moved forward in the frame and, passing along the groove, forced the cylinder to rotate one-sixth of a turn to align a chamber with the barrel. As the hammer was released to fire, the pin returned down a straight leg of the groove, so that it not only repositioned itself for the next shot but also acted as a cylinder lock, preventing the cylinder from turning during the hammer's fall.

When all six shots had been fired, a ring beneath the frame was pulled, unlocking a latch and allowing the barrel and cylinder to be hinged up, on a pivot just in front of the hammer. After moving clear the barrel came up against a stop

Mauser M1878 showing the characteristic zig-zag grooving on the cylinder

MAUSER M1878 ZIG-ZAG REVOLVER

This revolver was developed by Mauser in the hope of securing military adoption, but this did not take place and they were then sold on the civil market. They could be found in 7.6-mm, 9-mm and 10.6-mm calibres. The name Zig-Zag came from the grooving on the cylinder; a stud in the lower part of the frame, controlled by the hammer, moved back and forth in this grooving and so revolved the cylinder for each shot. Single action and double-action models were made, but they were not very popular and were not manufactured for very long

Weight: 1 lb 10½ oz	
Muzzle velocity: (10.6-mm) 700 fps	
Cylinder: 6 shots	

Peter Paul Mauser, head of one of the great German arms dynasties

on the standing breech and was held, but further pulling on the ring catch now operated a cam which thrust a central star plate out of the cylinder and simultaneously ejected all the empty cases. As in all Mauser products, the workmanship and finish were impeccable, but the military purchasers shied away from such an ingenious design. It was sure to go wrong in the hands of soldiers. Instead, they appointed a commission to look into revolver design.

The design that emerged was, by comparison with the Mauser, a prehistoric monster, but doubtless the commission felt it would survive rough handling in the field. This big,

ENFIELD .476 MARK I

This was the first British government-designed revolver, brought about by the problems of obtaining standardised weapons on the open market. It used an odd ejection system in which the barrel hinged down and the cylinder ran forward, away from the ejecting plate. This meant that the bottom cartridge case usually jammed in the frame. A Mark II was developed in 1882 and the pistol remained in use until the 1890s, being replaced by a Webley design

| Weight: 2 lb 9 oz |
| Muzzle velocity: 750 fps |
| Cylinder: 6 shots |

heavy solid frame revolver was in 10.6 mm calibre with a single-action lock. It was gate-loaded from the right but, surprisingly, there was no extraction system other than removing the cylinder arbor pin and the cylinder, and then using the pin to punch the cases from the chambers. With a 180 mm barrel, this was introduced in 1879 as the Reichs-revolver M79 or Trooper's Model and it was followed by the M83 or Officer's Model, which was more or less the same but lighter and with the barrel shortened to 125 mm. Precisely who was responsible for the design has never been publicly admitted; the revolvers were built by a consortium of makers in Suhl, the traditional gunmaking town in Thuringia.

Almost as anonymous was the French service revolver. This was made by the Manufacture d'Armes de St Etienne, but just who designed it is not certain. Again, conservatism won the day, and although St Etienne held patents for a simultaneous ejecting system, the Modèle 1873 was gate-loaded and used a rod ejector housed under the barrel in similar style to the Colt Frontier. In 11-mm calibre, it was effective enough.

In Britain the Army was short of revolvers in 1879 and had to go on to the civil market to buy 500 pistols of three different types, 20% of which were returned to the makers after being found defective. This was no way to equip an army, it was decided, and the Royal Small Arms Factory at Enfield was ordered to produce a design. Only 16 days later it had produced drawings and had them approved: one suspects that the factory had already been working on the design for a considerable time. The first models were tested in January, 1880, and the design was approved the following August, entering service as the Pistol Revolver, Breech Loading, Enfield, Mark 1.

There were odd things about the Enfield, but none more odd than the ejecting system, based on the patents of Owen Jones, of Philadelphia. The revolver was a hinged-frame model, the barrel hinging down, but instead of the cylinder moving with the barrel it remained on a plane parallel with the frame. The arbor was fixed to the standing breech, and a fixed extractor plate was attached to the arbor. As the barrel moved down, the cylinder was drawn straight forward on the arbor while the star plate remained in place, holding the rims of the cartridge cases. In effect, the cylinder was drawn off the cases, rather than the cases ejected from the cylinder.

The only defect with this system was that the bottom case usually stuck between the frame and the star plate and the cylinder had to be revolved by hand to clear it. Another interesting feature was that the movement of the cylinder was just sufficient to allow a fired case to come free of the chamber, but if any cartridge had not been fired, then it would not fall out since the bullet was still lodged inside the chamber. Thus ejection was selective, only fired cases being thrown clear.

Other features of the Enfield included rifling at the front of the chambers to start the bullet revolving before it reached the barrel, and nickel-plating of the internal parts of the lock. Experience showed that these two features were not as desirable in practice as in theory; the chamber rifling tended to choke with lead flakes from the bullets, and the nickel-plating tended to peel and jam the mechanism. Corrections were made before quantity production began.

But the Enfield was never wholly satisfactory, the principal complaint being that accuracy soon fell away. An attempt to

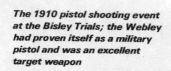
The 1910 pistol shooting event at the Bisley Trials; the Webley had proven itself as a military pistol and was an excellent target weapon

cure this was made in the Mark 2, in 1881, which had the forward end of the chambers taper-bored and also had some other mechanical refinements, but still nobody was very happy with the weapon. It was chambered for the .476 Eley cartridge, a round with good stopping power but poor accuracy in any weapon, though it was some time before this was realised.

Meanwhile the brothers Joseph and Philip Webley, of Birmingham, had been quietly building up a trade in revolvers, having begun making percussion weapons in the 1850s. At first they had a hard time of it, since Colonel Colt had set a factory in London to produce his revolvers and the Webleys could not compete with the prices Colt was able to charge for his mass-produced weapons. But in 1856 Colt closed his

Radio Times Hulton

200Y

WEBLEY-PRYSE

One of the most important features of the Webley-Pryse of 1877 was this system of securely locking the top strap. Two spring-loaded arms carry locking bolts which pass through the side of the standing breech and into the top strap. Only by pressing both bolts open at the same time could the revolver be opened for re-loading. One of the most secure systems ever devised, this lock was widely copied in later years and used with the heaviest revolvers

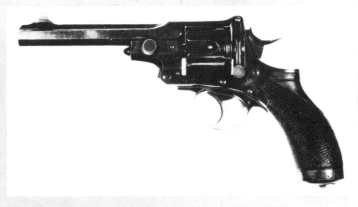

London factory, and the Webleys began to make more progress with their revolvers. In 1867 they made their first important model, which was adopted by the Royal Irish Constabulary as their standard sidearm and thus became known as the RIC model. In later years it was also adopted widely by police and military forces throughout the British Empire, and it can fairly be considered as the cornerstone of Webley's subsequent fame and fortune.

The RIC model was a solid-frame revolver of heavy calibre and compact proportions which soon acquired a reputation for robustness. Originally in .442 calibre, variant models were made in .45, .455, .476 and .430 chambering for both the service and civilian markets. Evidence of its popularity and reputation is the widespread copying of the basic style by

WEBLEY .455 SERVICE REVOLVER

Webley supplied the Army with revolvers from 1892 until after the First World War. The sectioned drawing shows the robust mechanism and the hinged-frame construction with auto-ejection as the barrel was broken open

Weight: 2 lb 2 oz	
Muzzle velocity: 650 fps	
Cylinder: 6 shots	

TRADE MARK

W & S.

Belgian makers, who invariably called them Constabulary Type revolvers in their advertising.

Although Webleys continued to make the RIC until the late 1890s, and also made a variety of other solid-frame revolvers – notably their Army Express model – their fame was to be ensured by their adoption of a hinged-frame design. After some experimental starts in this direction, in 1877 they marketed the Webley-Pryse revolver, the name coming from their adoption of features patented by Charles Pryse the Younger. The hinged frame had been adopted by Webley after a patent by Edward Wood, but the adoption of the Pryse ideas lifted the design out of the common run. The first improvement was the rebounding hammer; Pryse so designed his lockwork that after a shot had been fired, and the finger was relaxed on the trigger, the mainspring lifted the hammer away from the cylinder to almost the half-cock position, so that no accidental blow on the hammer could possibly fire the pistol. Moreover, it was now safe to carry the pistol with all chambers loaded, a hazardous proposition in earlier designs.

The method of rotating and locking the cylinder was also improved, and an obvious feature was the double-bolt locking of the top strap (over the cylinder) to the standing breech. These two bolts entered from each side of the breech and were withdrawn, to open the pistol, by pressing two spring-loaded levers which ran down behind the cylinder. As the pistol was opened, a star plate extractor was forced from the centre of the cylinder to eject the empty cases. A final identifying point was the cylinder lock, a milled knob beneath the barrel on the left side of the pistol. Rotating this through 180° released the cylinder so that it could be slipped from the arbor for cleaning once the gun had been opened.

Unfortunately, Webley did not have the monopoly of Pryse's patents, and they were licensed to a number of other gunmakers, notably August Francotte, of Liège. As a result it is not always easy to determine whether a Pryse is a Webley-Pryse, but there is no doubt that the Webley models were made in larger numbers than were any of the competitors and they were widely bought by Army officers.

Sound as the Pryse frame-locking system was – and it was widely copied, both with and without benefit of licence – it was not ideal for military service, particularly service cavalry, since it needed two hands to operate, one holding the revolver and the other pressing in the two spring-locking arms. Webley

decided to design an arm primarily for military use, in the hopes of securing a Government contract; he had, after all, considerable experience of supplying revolvers privately to officers, and their comments no doubt guided him. The most significant change was a new method of locking the frame and barrel together, by a hinged latch which sprang over the end of the top strap and which could be released by thumb-pressure of the firing hand on the tail of the catch itself. Moreover, the position of the catch, above the standing breech, was such that unless it was properly latched the hammer was intercepted and could not fall far enough for the firing pin to strike the cap of the cartridge in the chamber. This completely obviated the danger of 'blowing open' which had previously been an occasional hazard with all makes of hinged-frame revolvers. And, of course, it was now possible for a cavalryman to open his revolver with his firing hand while controlling his horse with the other; how he reloaded was, apparently, another question.

Otherwise, the basic layout of the revolver was much the same as the Webley-Pryse, and such features as the rebounding hammer and the cylinder lock were carried over into the new design. An innovation was the addition of a cam to the extracting mechanism which, after forcing the star plate out to eject the cases, allowed it to snap back as the revolver was fully opened, so that it could be re-loaded without danger of the new rounds falling out; previous models did not return the star plate until the revolver was closed, and reloading had to be done rather carefully.

After exhaustive tests, the Webley design was formally approved in 1887, though issues did not begin until 1892. The Mark 1 model was in .442 calibre, had a 4 in barrel, a six-shot cylinder, and weighed 34 oz loaded. It was an immediate success; Webley was given a contract for 10,000 revolvers, worth £30,500, and this was followed by contracts for various foreign governments, police forces and other official bodies. The Webley revolver, with minor modifications from time to time, was to remain in British service until after the Second World War.

While the big names creamed off the military contracts, there were plenty of smaller companies who could make a satisfactory living from the civilian market. In those far-off days when no permits were needed and no moral stigma was attached to ownership of a hand gun, this market was very large indeed, and the result was a wide variety of pocket revolvers. In this atmosphere such names as Harrington & Richardson, Hopkins & Allen and Iver Johnson in America, Pickert in Germany, Raick Frères, Robar and Francotte of Belgium, and innumerable 'country gunmakers' in England came to be associated with every type of solid frame, hinged-frame, auto-ejecting or non-ejecting revolver in calibres from .22 short to .45. Even to tabulate them would take pages, and in spite of their having generally been made down to a price rather than up to a standard, they functioned well enough for their intended purpose of self-defence, and, surprisingly, many of them are still capable of functioning.

By the middle 1880s, though, a number of inventors were a little tired of the revolver; it seemed to have reached the acme of perfection and there was little scope for inventiveness, all the good ideas having been patented and put to use. So inventive minds began to ask whether perhaps there wasn't some other way of making a hand gun work.

Mechanical Repeaters: Dead End Development

Round about this time the bolt-action repeating rifle had begun to find its place in the military world, and the bolt action became the new handgun mechanism, which led to a complete new group of weapons. For various reasons they did not last long, as a result of which they appear never to have collected a specific title, but they can conveniently be called the mechanical repeating pistols. One of the first to appear was that of Josef Schulhof, of Vienna, who in 1884 patented a pistol that used a sliding bolt operated by a trigger that ended in a finger-ring, so that it could be pushed as well as pulled. The butt grip of the pistol could be opened, and six cartridges placed inside, from whence they fed up a tube to the breech. The firer then grasped the pistol in the usual way, placed his forefinger inside the trigger ring and pushed forward. This drew the bolt back and allowed a cartridge to enter the feedway behind the breech. Pulling back on the trigger now closed the bolt and, by cams, rotated it to lock into the breech. As the bolt went forward a firing pin, contained inside, was cocked. Finally, an additional rearward squeeze of the trigger after the bolt had been locked would release the striker to fire the cartridge. A thrust with the forefinger now opened the bolt and ejected the spent case, and the cycle was repeated.

Two years later, in 1886, two more mechanical designs appeared. The first was from Paul Mauser and instead of using the reciprocating action of a bolt, it used the hinge-down action breechblock of the Martini rifle, together with a tubular magazine under the barrel. A forward thrust of the ring trigger lowered the breech block and collected a cartridge, spring-propelled out of the tubular magazine. A rearward pull on the trigger now lifted the cartridge and rammed it, then closed the breechblock by hinging it up, and finally dropped a hammer to fire the round via a firing pin in the breechblock. The mechanism was a watchmaker's nightmare of levers, cranks and cams, and, so far as is known, the pistol never got beyond the prototype stage.

The second 1886 model was by Karel Krnka, a Bohemian designer greatly given to odd mechanisms, and it used the reciprocating bolt but mounted a rotating magazine similar to a revolver cylinder, in the feedway. This magazine was simply a spindle with spring fingers holding the cartridges, so that the closing bolt could push a cartridge out of the fingers and into the breech. A few of these pistols were made, but they appear not to have achieved great commercial success.

The basic reasons for the failure of the mechanical repeater to catch on were simple; firstly, they were complicated devices, difficult to make and therefore expensive, at a time when sound revolvers could be bought for as little as 30s. Secondly, they asked too much of the human forefinger, which is not well designed for exerting a forward push. With the mechanism perfectly adjusted and lubricated, the guns worked sweetly, but to make them work when they were fouled with gunpowder residue, poorly lubricated, and fed with ammunition of varying quality which might jam in the chamber, was asking too much.

Moreover, while the mechanical repeater was trying to make itself known, a firearms revolution had taken place. Hiram Maxim had demonstrated that the energy wasted in a fired cartridge could, if properly utilised make a firearm self-actuating. All the human operator had to do with Maxim's

Schulhof 8-mm Model 1884. The ring trigger operates the bolt: the firing trigger is behind it

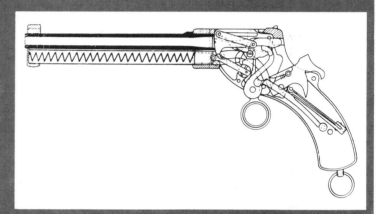

Mauser Mechanical Repeater, 1886. It is doubtful if any of these mechanical exercises were made

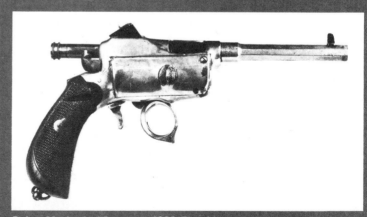

Reiger Mechanical Repeater, 1886. The side cover slides back to reveal the rotary magazine

machine-gun was feed a belt of ammunition into it and pull the trigger, whereupon the gun would proceed to load, fire, extract and reload until either the operator got tired and released the trigger or the gun ran out of ammunition. If it was possible to do this with a machine-gun, then there appeared to be no good reason why it could not be done with a handgun. And if it could, then there was no point in the mechanical repeater.

Ian Hogg

THE AGE OF THE AUTOMATIC

Attempts had been made to produce automatic hand-guns in the past; perhaps the best was a revolver made by Orbea, of Eibar, the Spanish gunmaking centre, in 1863. This used a port in the barrel to tap off some of the gas behind the bullet and channel it into a cylinder beneath, where it drove a piston backwards. By an arrangement of levers, this rotated the cylinder, cocked the hammer and ejected the empty case. But it was a one-off device that was never put on the market. The principal drawback to this, and to other attempts, was the ammunition. The early cartridges were made of spirally-wrapped brass, they were filled with gunpowder, and they carried soft lead bullets. As a result, the cases could not withstand the violent stresses of mechanical loading, the powder left thick fouling on the mechanism and blocked gas ports, and the soft bullets were easily deformed during loading.

But by 1880 a new type of ammunition had begun to appear. The French chemist Vielle had invented smokeless powder, for a start. It wasn't really smokeless, just very much less smoky than gunpowder, and it also left much less residue and fouling. Then came Major Rubin, of the Swiss Army, who had been working on some new ideas in bullet construction. He was concerned with the metallic fouling left in rifle barrels by lead bullets, and he had finally arrived at a design in which the bullet had a core of lead, to provide the desired mass, but was shrouded in a harder metal jacket, usually nickel or gilding metal. This jacket was thin enough and soft enough to deform into the rifling accurately, but of such a hardness that it did not flake off and leave fouling in rifle barrels. With the addition of the drawn brass cartridge case, the modern round of ammunition became a practical possibility, a round which was robust enough to withstand mechanical loading, and which did not clog up the gun's mechanism with filth.

Admittedly, there were still problem areas; the early smokeless powders tended to vary from batch to batch, so that the velocity and power delivered by the cartridge tended to vary, and the technique of drawing brass in such small dimensions but in vast quantities was still in its early days, leading to variations in the ductility of the brass. But by and large, the jacketed bullet, smokeless powder, drawn case combination was able to provide a cartridge far superior to anything that had gone before.

With ammunition of this class capable of being designed and manufactured, the way was clear for the development of automatic pistols. As we have seen, all this happened just about the time that the mechanical repeater was trying to make itself felt, and it was, in fact, a mechanical repeater which opened the door to the automatic pistol and, by doing so put the final nail in the mechanical pistol's coffin.

In 1890 Josef Laumann, of Vienna, took out patents for a mechanical repeater of the usual bolt-action, finger-operated type. He made some modifications in a second patent of 1891, but then, in a patent obtained in 1892 he changed the entire concept, doing away with the finger-trigger and introducing a unique system of operation which has never since been used in a handgun.

When any firearm is discharged, the explosion of the propelling charge inside the cartridge builds up high pressure which forces the bullet out of the barrel. Ignition is done by striking a light metal cap in the rear end of the cartridge; a sensitive compound inside the cap is nipped by the firing pin and caused to ignite, sending a flash through a tiny hole into the body of the case and thus firing the powder. Obviously, if flash goes forward through these tiny holes, pressure can come back, and the manufacturers of cartridges take pains to fix the percussion cap very securely in the base of the case. Moreover, the designer of the pistol also ensures that the breech is tight against the case to prevent the cap being blown back by the pressure inside the case – which in handguns can be up to four or five tons to the square inch – and thus jamming the mechanism. It was this set back of the cap that Laumann now used to operate his automatic pistol. The bolt was actuated by a forked arm, hinged at the bottom of the pistol frame and driven by a spring to force the bolt home. As the bolt went home, a lug on the arm lodged behind a recess in the frame to lock the bolt securely in place. The heavy firing pin carried a cam, and when the pistol fired, the cartridge cap set back about .18 of an inch, forcing the firing pin back so that the cam dislodged the locking lug and released the bolt. The residual pressure inside the cartridge case was then sufficient to drive the bolt back against the pressure of the arms and its spring. The spring would then return the bolt, which pushed the topmost cartridge out of the magazine and into the breech; the striker was cocked, and the bolt was locked behind the cartridge ready for the next shot.

Laumann took his design to the Austrian Arms Company, of Steyr, from whence, in 1892, it was marketed as the Schonberger automatic pistol; Schonberger was the superintendent of the Steyr factory, and just how his name came to be applied to the pistol is by no means clear. It is possible that it was a *quid pro quo* for production facilities. Nevertheless, the Schonberger goes down in history as the first automatic pistol on sale. It was 8-mm calibre and used a fairly powerful cartridge which has been estimated to have had a muzzle velocity around 1200 ft per second; only estimated, because nobody alive today has ever seen a Schonberger cartridge – they went off the market before the turn of the century.

Before moving further into pistol development, we should make one thing clear, and that is the precise definition of automatic pistol as opposed to its popular definition. Strictly speaking an automatic gun of any sort – pistol, rifle or machine-gun – is a gun which, once the trigger is pressed, will fire and go on firing until either the trigger is released or the gun runs out of ammunition. There have been a number of pistols, properly called automatic, which meet this definition. But the vast majority of pistols called automatic do not meet the definition at all; when the trigger is pressed, they fire one shot and that is all. No more will be fired until the firer releases his grip on the trigger and takes a fresh pull to fire the next shot. Indeed, the designers go to great lengths to ensure that automatic fire is prevented. Strictly speaking, these should be called self-loading pistols, and, indeed, in military terminology they often are. But for every person who calls them self-loaders, ten thousand call them automatics, and since the term is commonplace and convenient, we will continue to use it in these pages, though strictly it is incorrect. Where pistols of the true automatic type turn up, this will be made clear, and we will see that the manufacturers frequently gave them some title to distinguish them from the others.

Schonberger's pistol achieved a small degree of success, probably because it was a novelty, but it was not the great

Ian Hogg

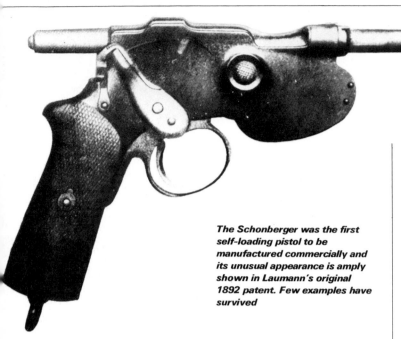

The Schonberger was the first self-loading pistol to be manufactured commercially and its unusual appearance is amply shown in Laumann's original 1892 patent. Few examples have survived

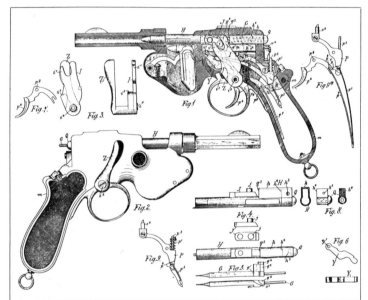

sales triumph that he appears to have hoped, and Schonberger pistols are exceedingly scarce today. But he had shown the way, and it was not long before others were crowding along behind him. And the next to appear on sale was the Borchardt.

Hugo Borchardt was born in Germany and at 16 emigrated to the United States, where he took American citizenship in about 1875. He worked for the Winchester company and designed several excellent revolvers. But none was put on the market; they were used more as bargaining counters. At that time, the story goes, Colt were contemplating putting a lever-action rifle on the market in direct competition with Winchester. Winchester, therefore, let it be known to Colt that they had some excellent revolver designs ready to put on the market in competition with Colt; and there is little doubt that the Winchester revolver would have made more of a dent in Colt's sales than the Colt rifle would have done with Winchester's. So an agreement was reached; Colt stayed out of the rifle market, and Winchester stayed out of the pistol market, and that's the way it has been ever since.

It may have been good business, but it was frustrating to Borchardt, and in about 1882 he went to work for the Royal Hungarian Arms Factory in Budapest. Here he apparently saw the Maxim machine-gun during its demonstrations in Austria in 1888 and was impressed by its toggle-lock. He

began to design a pistol and rifles using this lock, but he could see little prospect of its being adopted by the Austro-Hungarian War Department. In about 1890 he offered his ideas to Ludwig Löwe & Co, of Berlin. This company had begun in 1864, making sewing machines, and then became one of the foremost manufacturers of machinery. In the 1870s they had made licensed copies of the Smith & Wesson .44 Russian revolver for sale in Europe, and later held large government contracts for Mauser rifles. The company hired him as a designer and allowed him to carry on with the development of his pistol. In September, 1893, he took out his first German patents, followed by similar patents in Britain and the US, and in 1894 the Borchardt pistol was put on sale.

The Borchardt pistol was constructed with a butt and frame unit supporting a barrel and barrel extension unit. In the barrel extension lay the bolt, capable of sliding back and forth, and controlled by a toggle joint assembly. This consisted of two levers, the front one pivoted to the bolt and the rear one pivoted to a trunnion at the end of the barrel extension. The two were joined by a pivot which lay about midway between the bolt and the trunnion and was slightly below a line drawn between the bolt pivot and the trunnion. As a result, any rearward pressure on the bolt from firing the cartridge would tend to make the centre pivot move downward, press against the floor of the barrel extension, and resist any opening tendency of the bolt.

The rear section of the toggle did not end at its pivot on the trunnion; it extended a short distance behind and was terminated in a roller. A short distance behind this roller the pistol frame curved up and over, and a hardened steel cam path lay behind the roller. Finally, the frame end was bulbous and carried a curved, clock-type leaf spring, the free end of which was hooked to the underside of the rear section of the toggle, just behind its central joint.

When the pistol was fired the recoil force drove the barrel and barrel extension back, sliding across the top of the frame, and during this brief movement the bullet left the barrel and the breech pressure began to drop. As the recoiling portion came to the back of the frame, so the roller at the rear end of the toggle unit struck the cam surface in the back of the frame, and the shape of this surface forced down the rear end of the toggle and this lifted the front end and broke the central joint.

Once this central joint moved above the thrust line, there was no longer any resistance to the rearward movement of the bolt. At this point the barrel and extension stopped moving, but the bolt was free to go back, forced back by the pressure due to the momentum of the cartridge case. The toggle rose sufficiently to permit the bolt to extract the case and eject it; at the same time, it pulled on the leaf spring, and movement came to a stop when the rising rear toggle struck the rear end of the frame. Then the leaf spring reasserted itself and pulled the toggle down so that the bolt movement was reversed; the bolt ran forward, picking up a fresh cartridge from the box magazine in the butt and placing it in the chamber. The toggle came down, the joint dropping below the thrust line once more, and the bolt was securely locked. A striker inside the bolt was cocked during the return stroke, and all was ready for the next shot.

In the 80 years which have passed since the Borchardt was first demonstrated, much adverse comment has been passed.

It has been said that it is cumbersome, delicate, sensitive to its ammunition and so forth. These remarks are, to some extent, justified, but only when applied with hindsight. Putting oneself in Borchardt's place, it is difficult to see how else he could have managed it, wedded as he was to the toggle lock. After all, Borchardt had little to guide him other than his own ingenuity; he was working in a completely new field. Indeed, he later said that he could get nowhere until he had perfected the round of ammunition, which, in itself, was a major design achievement. The peculiar demands of an automatic mechanism, subjecting the cartridge to unheard-of stresses in the fraction of a second's action of loading, plus subjecting it to a considerable battering as it sat in the magazine, because of the recoil, were not met by any existing revolver ammunition, and Borchardt, aided by one Georg Luger, another employee of the Löwe company, and by technicians of the Deutsche Metallpatronenfabrik (a part of Löwe at that time) started from scratch. They based their work on contemporary rifle ammunition, coming up with a jacketed bullet, bottle-necked rimless cartridge case design filled with smokeless powder. By present-day standards it was pretty unreliable, since in those days smokeless powder technology was in its infancy and performance from shot to shot was not consistent; but by the standards of the day it was a remarkable advance, and it was vital to the pistol's success.

The Borchardt C/93 pistol, in 7.65-mm calibre, was supplied with a wooden butt-stock which could be screwed to the rear of the frame to turn the pistol into a moderately useful carbine. The barrel was 165 mm long, and the sights were graduated to 700 metres, a trifle optimistic, though it is possible to make good practice up to about 200 yards. About 800 Borchardt pistols were made by Löwe between 1894 and 1896, and these are marked Waffenfabrik Löwe over the chamber, and System Borchardt Patent on the frame. In 1896 the Löwe empire was reorganised and became the Deutsche Waffen- und Munitionsfabriken (DWM) and the subsequent production, estimated at about 2200 pistols, bore the DWM name in full on the frame.

Although 3000 pistols in about six years is a small production, the Borchardt made a greater impact than had the Schonberger, and several important arms firms began to look more closely at the automatic pistol. In fact, one maker had been working on designs for much the same time as had Borchardt, and placed pistols on the market at almost the same time; this was Theodor Bergmann, whose Model 1894 began a long series of Bergmann automatics.

Bergmann has been spoken of as a great designer and innovator, but recent research has shown that he did not in fact design anything very important. He was a manufacturer and salesman who had the good sense to hire a first-class designer, Louis Schmeisser, and then, in the accepted German business practice, patent Schmeisser's designs under the company name. The Bergmann M1894 pioneered the blow-back system, in which the recoil force on the base of the cartridge, because of the gas pressure, blew the bolt back without any form of restraint or locking other than the resistance of a return spring. Where the bullet was small, the charge light, and the mass of the bolt relatively large, this system worked well, and still does, and Bergmann made his pistol in 5-mm, 6.5-mm and 8-mm calibres.

The mechanical arrangements were somewhat odd, but

BORCHARDT 7.65-mm MODEL 1893

This was the first automatic pistol to be successful on the commercial market. It was the first to use the toggle lock and the first to house the magazine inside the butt. In this sectioned drawing the action of the toggle can be determined; on recoil the end of the toggle is directed down by the casing behind the frame, which causes the centre of the toggle to rise and unlock the breech. The return spring is a clock-type leaf spring in the rear casing. A detachable butt-stock could be screwed to the spring casing to make the pistol into a passable carbine. It is reliably estimated that slightly more than 3000 Borchardt pistols were made between 1893 and 1899

| Weight: 2 lb 14 oz |
| Muzzle velocity: 1310 fps |
| Magazine: 8 rounds |

The Borchardt was also available with a detachable stock making a functional if inelegant carbine

BERGMANN 6.5-mm MODEL 1896

The Bergmann, designed by Louis Schmeisser, was the first pistol to popularise the blow-back system of operation. It used a simple square-section bolt, which blew back on the frame to re-cock the external hammer, and the magazine was in front of the trigger, loaded by a special clip. The side cover of the magazine was hinged down to allow the clip to be dropped in. Although odd-looking to modern eyes, these early Bergmann pistols were a great novelty in their time and were extremely popular for 'saloon' target shooting. It was also known as the Bergmann No 3 model

| Weight: 1 lb 10 oz |
| Muzzle velocity: 800 fps |
| Magazine: 5 shots |

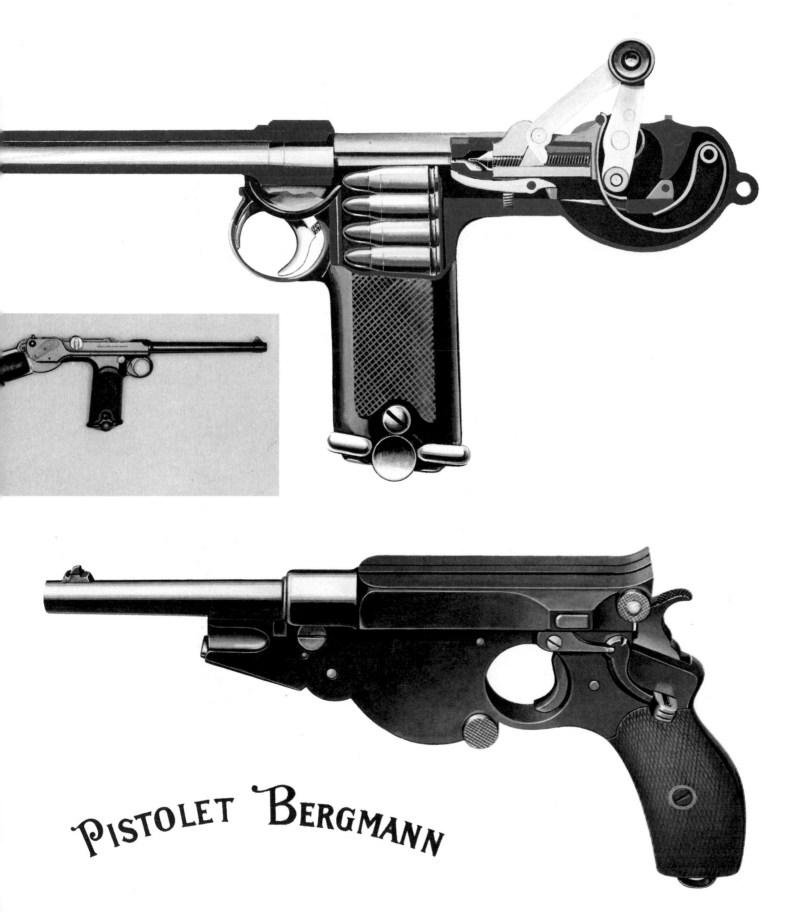

PISTOLET BERGMANN

again we should remember that they were designed at a time when there was no existing practice on which to base them; the recoil or return spring was placed beneath the bolt, while the magazine was in front of the trigger, loaded by clips and with the cartridges forced up by a follower arm. The clip could be dropped into the magazine so that a small loop protruded from the bottom, after which grasping the loop and pulling would drag out the clip, leaving the cartridges in the magazine. Alternatively, the clip could be left in place. In practice, it was better to leave the clip in place, since with it removed there was too much clearance inside the magazine and the cartridges jammed.

Another Bergmann innovation was the absence of an extractor and, indeed, the absence of any form of rim or groove on the cartridge case. The design relied on the gas pressure in the case not only to blow the bolt back but also to blow the empty case out of the chamber, when it would bounce off the next cartridge in the magazine and thus be ejected from the feedway. Again, this was a better idea on paper than it ever was in practice, the ejected cases generally refusing to bounce in the right direction and jamming the returning bolt.

Nevertheless, Bergmann's pistols sold very well; they were easy to shoot, since they used lightly-loaded cartridges; they could be had in a variety of barrel lengths and with target sights for competitive shooting, and the smaller ones fitted into a coat pocket. They were later improved, largely by adding an extraction rim to the cartridge and a positive extractor to the bolt, though their basic layout remained the same for many years, and they enjoyed a steady sale throughout the 1890s.

Few designers however gave much thought to the possibility of a civilian market, for home or personal defence or for target shooting. Their aim was to get their pistol accepted by a military body; once this was done, success was assured. The military would buy by the thousand, and military adoption was a cachet of respectability which would enable them to sell to other countries. The only difficulty was that the military were notoriously conservative; at that time they were wedded to revolvers, and for an automatic pistol to take over from the revolvers, it would have to be powerful. And power meant a locked breech, which in turn meant involved design. So Bergmann was out of the running in that field.

One gentleman with a lot of experience of military requirements was Mauser; his rifles were going from success to success, but he had failed to interest the German Army in his Zig-Zag revolver. So in 1894, seeing the Borchardt pistol, he decided it was time to look into the automatic pistol business and produce something firmly aimed at military use. As it happened, his factory manager, Herr Federle, had been working on a design for some time, assisted by his brothers. Mauser therefore called on him to develop the design for the company, and in March, 1895, the first prototype was ready. After some minor alterations, the Mauser pistol was patented in December, 1895, and the Borchardt was confronted with its first serious competition.

The Mauser was a much more effective design than the Borchardt. In later years Borchardt is said to have pointed out that Mauser's task was made easy by the fact that he took Borchardt's 7.65-mm cartridge as his basis and also had the Borchardt in front of him as a guide to the defects to be corrected. There may be some truth in this, but there is, equally, little doubt that the Federle brothers had worked out the basic principles before the Borchardt pistol appeared. True, Mauser appropriated the 7.65-mm Borchardt cartridge, though he made some minute alterations in its dimensions and put a more powerful charge inside it; he then called it the 7.63-mm Mauser so that there was no chance of mistaking one for the other, and in so doing he constructed one of the world's immortal cartridges.

The Mauser design was similar to the Borchardt in that it used a barrel and barrel extension sliding on top of the butt and frame unit, but the resemblance stopped there. The barrel extension, apart from an aperture behind the breech to allow loading and ejection, was a square-section tunnel, with the square-section bolt reciprocating within it. The bolt was hollow, with the return spring inside and also the striker and its spring, all held in place by a cross-key through the barrel extension. An external hammer was cocked as the bolt recoiled and was released by the trigger to fall on the rear end of the striker as it protruded from the bolt. The magazine was in front of a trigger-guard, a fixed box which held ten rounds, loaded in by stripping them in from a clip in similar fashion to the Mauser rifle technique.

Breech locking was done by a locking block pivoted to the barrel extension and provided with two lugs which engaged in two recesses in the bottom of the bolt. (The original design had one lug but this was soon changed to two.) This block was forced up by a ramp in the pistol frame, so when the barrel was forward, the block was engaged with the bolt and bolt, barrel and extension were all solidly locked together. When the pistol was fired, the barrel assembly recoiled far enough to let the bullet leave the barrel, after which the locking block slid free of its ramp and dropped clear of the bolt. At this point the rearward movement of the barrel and extension was stopped, and the bolt was free to continue its rearward movement, extracting the spent case and then returning, under the pressure of its spring, to chamber the next round. Once this was done the whole barrel unit moved forward again, pulling the block up on its ramp and bringing the lugs into engagement with the bolt. The whole system was extremely strong and reliable; it has never been known to fail and it stayed the same throughout the Mauser's long career.

The Mauser C/96 – frequently called the Military Model – had a 133-mm barrel and a 10-shot magazine; a few were made in 1897 with a 120-mm barrel and a six-shot magazine, but they did not sell as well as the larger weapon and few were made. An interesting point about these early models was than the backsight was a simple notch in the rear edge of the barrel extension, and the hammer was made with a large ring head which, when the hammer was uncocked, obscured the view of the backsight, thus reminding the firer that the pistol was not in a condition to fire unless he could get a clear view of the sights.

The C/96 was an immediate success on the commercial market, but it met with little encouragement from the military. Possibly in the hopes of achieving a more military image, the design was changed in 1898; the barrel became 140-mm long, the hammer head was made smaller and no longer obscured the sight; the backsight was adjustable to a maximum range of 700 metres; and the back edge of the butt

SCHWARZLOSE MODEL 1892

This was the first automatic pistol designed by Andreas Schwarzlose. It used a recoiling barrel and a breech block which swung down to collect a fresh cartridge from the oddly-arranged magazine beneath the barrel. An external hammer was hung on the same pivot as the breech-block and was cocked by the recoil stroke. No data can be given for this pistol since only one was ever made; it was in a Belgian museum before 1939 but has since disappeared

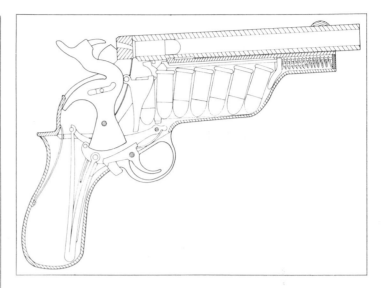

was grooved to take a wooden stock. This stock was, in fact, a beautifully-made wooden holster into which the pistol fitted, being mounted on a leather backing-piece for attachment to a belt. A metal tongue on the bottom of the holster allowed it to be clipped to the butt to turn the weapon into a carbine.

In spite of the improvements, military acceptance eluded the Mauser. It was taken into military use in Turkey, China, Persia, and the Italian Navy, but these were of little consequence compared to the boost which acceptance by a major European army would have meant. But for all that, the Mauser sold very well, by the tens of thousands, being bought by officers throughout Europe as well as by civilian shooters, and its success completely eclipsed the Borchardt.

The next important design to appear was from Andreas Schwarzlose; he was, at this time, relatively unknown, though in later years his machine-gun became the standard of the Austrian Army and remained in service until 1945. His first pistol design was patented in 1892 but was never made; in 1895 he patented a long-recoil design, which appears to have been the first of this breed. In this system the barrel and bolt recoil, locked together, for a distance somewhat greater than the length of a complete cartridge. The bolt is then unlocked and held fast, while the barrel is allowed to return to the forward position. Once it gets there, it releases the bolt, which then runs forward and chambers the next round. The system will be met again, and in one or two instances has achieved success, but it remains a rare method of operation, and in this instance it got nowhere.

Then in 1896 he produced his Military Model, which made up for his previous efforts. It was, potentially, a far better design than either the Borchardt or the Mauser, and if Schwarzlose had managed to get it into production three years earlier, and iron out some of the very minor design defects, he might very well have outshone both those designs. But the history of firearms is peppered with such 'ifs'.

The Schwarzlose 1896 was an elegant-looking pistol which fired the 7.63-mm Mauser cartridge. The bolt was locked by being rotated through 45° by a cam track in the frame, an efficient and neat system; the magazine was in the sloped butt; the bolt was held open after the last shot had been fired; and a positive ejector lever knocked the extracted round clear of the feedway. There were minor drawbacks; the extractor, for example, did not actually hook on to the cartridge case rim until the striker went forward, which made it difficult to extract an unfired round; and the holding-open device was complicated. But these points could have been easily rectified to make the Military a very fine pistol indeed. However, by the time it got to the market, the Mauser was well entrenched, and the demand for the Schwarzlose was so small that the designer apparently never felt it worth his while to make any improvements.

Schwarzlose pistols are rare today, and for a peculiar reason. It seems that a Berlin wholesaler had the entire stock of Schwarzlose pistols on his hands and was despairing of ever getting rid of them; then, in 1905, a bunch of Russian revolutionaries bought the remaining stock, possibly amounting to a thousand, for clandestine shipment to Russia. Unfortunately for them, the Russian police got wind of the plan and seized the shipment, after which they issued the pistols to police and customs guards. As a result, almost the entire supply of Schwarzlose pistols finished up in Russia, from whence few have returned.

In spite of the fact that there were by now three powerful automatic pistols available, no military contracts were forthcoming, and the reason for this was largely that all three had been designed by technicians who were concerned with the pistol as a mechanism, and not by soldiers concerned with it as a fighting machine. All three were long and cumbersome weapons, temperamental unless carefully looked after, not the sort to be manipulated quickly and instinctively in a tight corner. This was obvious, at any rate, to Georg Luger, and he set about rectifying it.

Georg Luger, the son of a dentist, became a cadet in the Austro-Hungarian Army at 16. Seven years later, in 1872, he left to marry and take up engineering, but those seven years had taught him a lot about the practicalities of firearms. In about 1875 he met von Mannlicher, a famous weapons designer, and they collaborated on the design of a rifle magazine. This seems to have awakened a latent talent in Luger, and although continuing to earn his living as a railway engineer, he began designing rifles, both magazine and automatic types. In 1891 he joined the Löwe company in Berlin, gradually becoming what amounted to a consultant designer.

Precisely what proportion Borchardt and Luger contributed to the redesign of the Borchardt pistol and to whose credit the final design lies, is something which experts have argued about for several years. At one time it was thought that Luger completely redesigned the Borchardt, against Borchardt's wishes. It now seems likely that there was a good deal of collaboration; that Borchardt himself made some of the first changes in the design; that Luger made a major contribution by redesigning the ammunition; and, finally, that Borchardt could see no further way of improving the pistol and left it to Luger from then on. Borchardt was probably the more inventive designer, but, like many good designers, once the thing was in production he was satisfied, and merely wanted to get busy on a new project. Luger, on the other hand, had a clearer conception of what constituted a practical weapon and had a greater degree of application and single-mindedness which led him to improve and refine until he got what he was after.

The first sign of improvement came with the submission of

The Mauser "Broomhandle"

MAUSER 7.63-mm MILITARY

This exploded view shows the components of the Mauser. One of the remarkable features of this pistol is that there are no screws or pins anywhere except the two which hold the wooden grips in place; all the mechanical parts fit by interlocking

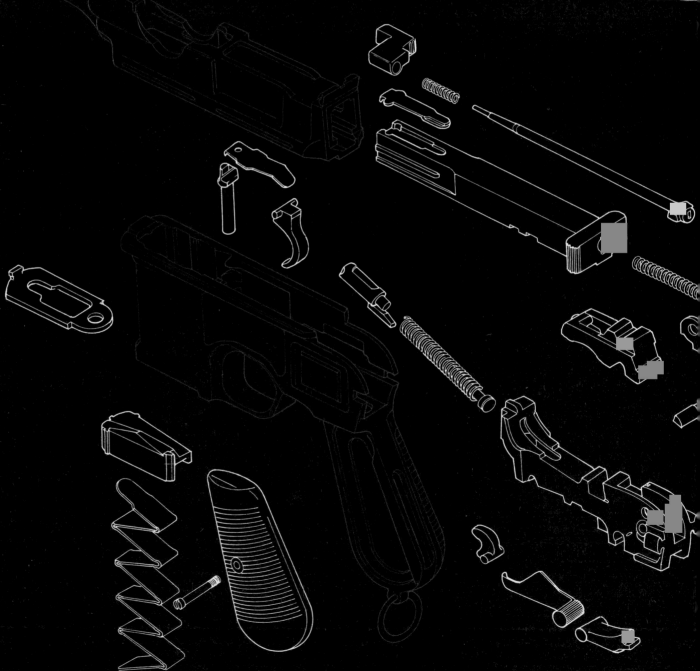

The Mauser 7.63-mm was also offered as a carbine with lengthened barrel, a graceful stock and wooden foregrip

MAUSER 7.63-mm MILITARY OR C/96

Another of the all-time famous pistols and next to the Luger, probably the most recognisable. This drawing shows the salient features of the design; the bolt, carried above the frame and locked by a two-lug locking unit below; the fixed magazine ahead of the trigger; the prominent hammer; and the odd grip which gave rise to the nickname 'Broomhandle'. It may look awkward but it is a powerful and accurate weapon which is capable of good shooting in the hands of someone used to it. With the wooden butt-holster fitted it can make good practice to ranges of 400 yards or so

Weight:	2 lb 11 oz
Muzzle velocity:	1420 fps
Magazine:	10 shots

National Army Museum

British officers who went to the Boer War largely bought their own pistols. This one, like the young war correspondent Winston Churchill favoured a Mauser C/96, to take to South Africa

ERFURT

The 'Luger' first adopted for military service by the Swiss in 1900 became one of the world's outstanding military firearms. This Gefreiter in France, May 1940, has a model '08 slung from the belt

a Borchardt-Luger pistol to the Swiss Army for trials in 1898. The shape had changed considerably; the overhang behind the butt, with the bulbous spring casing, had vanished, while the butt was now sloped at 55° to the body. Borchardt had changed his return spring to a flattened leaf laid down the rear of the grip and connected to the toggle by a bell-crank arrangement, while Luger had altered the toggle action by doing away with the rear overhang and roller, making the toggle break by having the centre joint strike an inclined ramp on the pistol frame. This cleaned up the whole shape of the pistol. In addition, the trigger mechanism had been improved and a grip safety device fitted into the rear edge of the butt, which meant the pistol could not be fired unless it was correctly held and the grip safety depressed.

The pistol's performance in the trial was good, but the Swiss requested some small changes, particularly a manual safety catch besides the grip safety device. The breechblock was slightly redesigned to obtain smoother action, and the frame was slightly altered. But the greatest change was in the ammunition. The Swiss felt that the 7.65-mm Borchardt cartridge was too powerful, so Luger shortened it. This reduced the power, made the pistol more controllable and accurate, and allowed the pistol to be redesigned with a shorter operating stroke of the toggle. The new cartridge became the 7.65-mm Parabellum, since Parabellum was the trade-mark and telegraphic address of DWM in Berlin. With all these improvements incorporated, the pistol was re-submitted to the Swiss in 1899, was accepted, and on May 4, 1900, the Swiss officially adopted the Pistol, Ordonnanz 1900, System Borchardt-Luger.

While Luger had thus been getting his foot into the door of military approval, other people had also been busy. Von Mannlicher first showed interest in pistols in 1894 when he patented a peculiar blow-forward design; in this the barrel was free to slide forward, away from a standing breech, behind which was a conventional hammer. A return spring around the barrel kept it pressed against the breech. To load, the barrel was pulled forward, where it was held by a catch.

Then a clip of five 8-mm cartridges was placed into the open action and the rounds pressed from the clip into the magazine in the butt. The clip was removed and the trigger pressed. This released the catch and allowed the barrel to be driven back by its spring, collecting a cartridge from the magazine and bringing up against the standing breech. The hammer could then be thumbed back and dropped by pressing the trigger again, or continued pressure of the trigger would lift the hammer and then drop it to fire the cartridge. On firing, the torque of the bullet and its friction in the barrel, together with the residual pressure in the chamber pushing back on the case, all tended to throw the barrel forward; an extractor pulled the case away as the barrel left it, and ejected the case. The barrel then stopped in the forward position, waiting for the firer to release the trigger, where-upon the barrel would run back to chamber the next round. Apart from its mechanical novelty, there was little to commend the design, and it does not appear to have been put on sale.

Having got that out of his system, von Mannlicher patented something rather less exotic in 1896, though as he did not put it into production until some years later it is more often called the Model 1903. It resembled the Mauser in its general arrangement, having a similar barrel, extension and bolt, and a similar magazine in front of the trigger. But the locking system was much simpler, a strut which hinged up from the rear of the extension to wedge itself behind the bolt, forced up by a block on the frame. Not only was it simpler, it was also less strong than the Mauser system; Mannlicher chambered the pistol for a 7.65-mm round of his own design which was dimensionally similar to the Borchardt and Mauser rounds but weaker than either. One result of this was mechanical disaster when anybody tried to fire a Mauser cartridge in a Mannlicher pistol, a circumstance which did little to enhance the Mannlicher's reputation. This pistol was entered for the Swiss trials in 1898 but did not impress the Swiss.

Finally, in 1898, von Mannlicher took out a patent, for a

PISTOLE PARABELLUM 9-mm M1908

The Parabellum P'08 universally known after its designer Georg Luger is one of the most famous handguns of them all. The earlier Borchardt had introduced the toggle-lock but Luger refined the system into a far less cumbersome weapon. The toggle-lock depended on consistent ammunition quality and exposed its working parts as it rose and fell on firing – nevertheless it was widely used by the German armed forces in two world wars and was widely exported

Weight: 1 lb 14 oz	
Muzzle velocity: 1150 fps	
Magazine: 8 shots	

The first military Parabellum – the Swiss 7.65-mm Ordonnanzpistole of 1900

MANNLICHER 7.6-mm M1894

This unusual pistol was one of the first designs of von Mannlicher to go on sale. It is a blow-forward pistol rather than a blow-back; the breech is fixed to the frame and the force of the explosion, plus the drag of the bullet, pulls the barrel forward on the frame. It is then returned by a spring, collecting a fresh round nose-first as it does so. A system of levers beneath the barrel ejects the spent case and also cocks the hammer after each shot. It is believed that fewer than 100 were made

Weight: 1 lb 10 oz
Muzzle velocity: 850 fps
Magazine: 6 shots

delayed blowback pistol. This was extremely elegant and well-balanced, one of the most beautiful pistols ever made. It used a fixed barrel and a simple recoiling breechblock which was delayed by the pressure of a long leaf spring pressing against its lower edge. The magazine was inside the butt and was loaded through the open action by a clip. It was chambered for a new 7.65-mm Mannlicher cartridge which had straight sides and was not interchangeable with any other pistol round of the period, so that there could not be any unfortunate accidents. Although this Mannlicher M1901 was bought by Austrian and German officers on their own account, it failed to gain acceptance by any European army, though it later became the standard Argentine Army pistol.

Strangely, all this activity in Europe seems to have attracted little attention in the US, and the only American designer to take any interest in the automatic pistol was, not surprisingly, John M Browning. Browning had already developed a serviceable machine-gun for the US Army and was working on better ideas, but in the middle 1890s he decided to leave machine-guns for a time and look at pistols. In April 1897 he took out a number of patents covering blowback pistols and tried to interest Colt in them; but Colt were firmly wedded to revolvers and the only automatic pistol they were prepared to contemplate was a heavy weapon

suitable for military use. Browning therefore went to Belgium and negotiated a licence agreement with the Fabrique National d'Armes de Guerre, of Herstal, near Liège, under which they were free to develop the patents and market the pistols under the Browning name in the Eastern Hemisphere.

The Fabrique National had been formed some years earlier to manufacture Mauser rifles for the Belgian Army, so they had some knowledge of military requirements. But they were also shrewd enough to see what apparently nobody else had thought of: the huge potential civilian market for pocket pistols for home and personal defence. In those far-off days there were few restrictions on owning a pistol, and vast numbers of revolvers were sold for private use. Fabrique National reasoned that since the automatic pistol could be made much less bulky, this huge market could profitably be converted from revolvers to automatics.

Accordingly, they set to work on the Browning patents, and by 1898 they had produced a suitable design. It was a blowback, with the return spring mounted above the barrel inside a slide which acted as a shroud for the barrel, a container for the return spring, and as the breechblock, carrying a firing pin. The return spring pressed against the front interior of the slide and against a collar above the breech, attached to the fixed barrel. A rod, passing through the spring and attached to the front of the slide, had its rear end attached to a suspended arm which was hooked into the firing pin carrier. In this was the return spring also acted as a firing pin spring.

When the gun was fired, the slide was blown to the rear, and the rod pulled the spring, compressing it against the collar. As the slide was pulled back by the expansion of the spring, the firing pin carrier was held by a sear, part of the firing mechanism, and the hanging arm placed extra pressure on the spring. Pulling the trigger released the sear from the carrier, allowing the spring to pull the arm forward, which in turn pulled the carrier and firing pin on to the cartridge.

A pistol of this type was sent to Switzerland for test by the Swiss Army but they were not interested, since the 7.65-mm cartridge (also designed by Browning) was much weaker than the Parabellum cartridge and not, in their view, suited to military service. Nothing daunted, Fabrique National made some minor improvements in the design and put it on the market in 1899. In March 1900 it was adopted by the Belgian Army – in spite of the small calibre and the blowback mechanism – and from then on sales mushroomed; a quarter of a million were sold in the next six years, more than every other automatic pistol in the world put together. Fabrique National's gamble had paid off handsomely.

The Model 1900 (or Old Model as it came to be called) was a good first attempt, and Fabrique National were not going to let it rest there. They proceeded to develop a much simpler design, which they produced as the Model 1903 or Modèle de Guerre. This reduced the automatic pistol to as basic and simple a format as has ever been devised consistent with reliability. The slide moved back and forth in rails milled in the pistol frame and carried a simple firing pin in its rear section. The barrel was loose, but retained in place on the frame by three lugs beneath the breech engaging in three recesses cut in the frame, just ahead of the trigger-guard. Beneath the barrel lay the return spring, its front end abutting against the front of the slide, its rear end against the pistol

BROWNING 7.65-mm MODEL 1900

This is the 'Old Model' Browning, the first to be placed on sale by Fabrique National of Liège. It was a blowback pistol, with the recoil spring concealed in the frame above the barrel. In this design, the recoil spring also acted as the striker spring, being hooked to the hammer at its rear end. Browning also developed the cartridge for this pistol, a cartridge which was to become the most popular one in the world for pocket automatic pistols

Weight: 1 lb 6½ oz

Muzzle velocity: 985 fps

Magazine: 7 shots

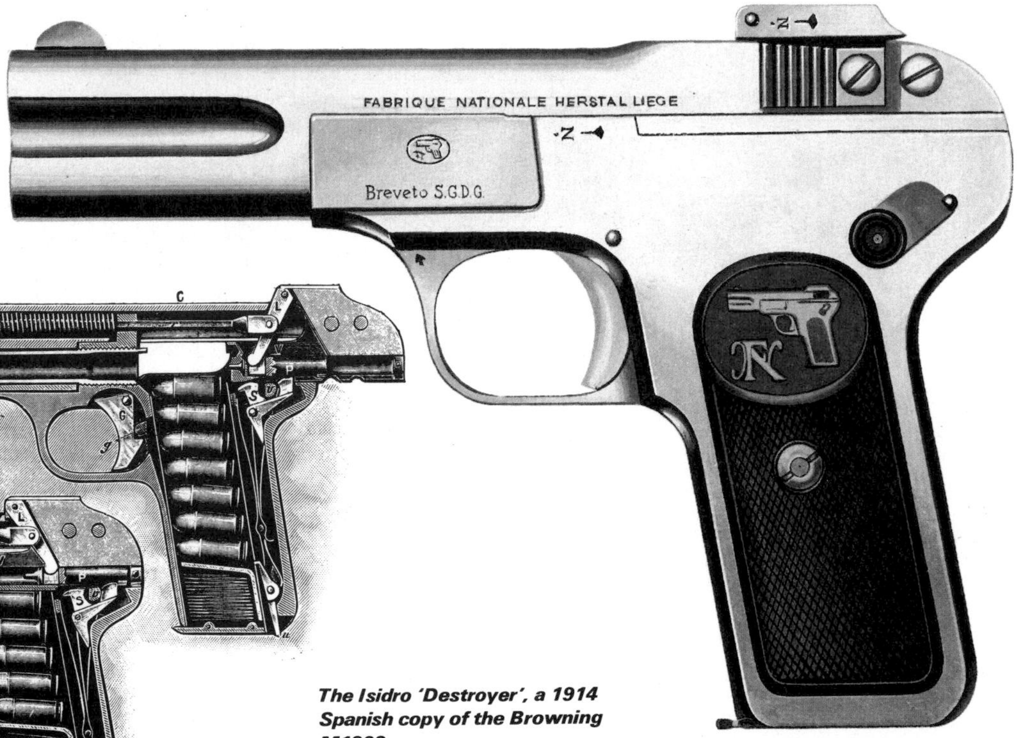

A French print of 1906 amply explains the elegantly simple mechanism of the Browning M1900

Mary Evans

The Isidro 'Destroyer', a 1914 Spanish copy of the Browning M1903

Ian Hogg

frame. Once the slide was in position on the frame, the barrel was firmly located; it could not move fore-and-aft because of the lugs engaged in the frame, nor could it revolve because of the internal contours of the slide. Firing was done by an internally-mounted hammer, and the pistol was chambered for a new cartridge, the 9-mm Browning Long.

The Model 1903 was an even greater success than the Old Model; the Belgian Army adopted it in place of the Old Model; the Swedish Army adopted it and, after Fabrique National stopped making it in 1923, continued to produce it until 1942. The 1903 was made in the hundreds of thousands, to such good effect that in many parts of Europe the word Browning became synonymous with automatic pistol. And for every one which Fabrique National made, a score or more were turned out by pirates.

The Basque town of Eibar had long been Spain's gun-making centre and scores of small factories produced every type of firearm. Few of these were to original design, because of the peculiar patent laws in Spain; broadly speaking, a design could not be patented in Spain unless it was actually on sale there, so an astute operator, working swiftly, could copy a foreign design and get it on sale before the foreigner, thus forestalling any application for a patent. This is what happened to the Browning 1903; the design was so simple

that it was God's gift to the Eibar gunshops, which relied on hand working by innumerable small contractors. By 1905 copies of the 1903 were appearing in Spain and they continued to appear in vast numbers until the early 1930s. There were one or two minor changes to suit the Spanish system of manufacture, and they were usually in 7.65-mm calibre rather than 9-mm Browning Long; some of them were as good as Brownings, most of them were of the cheapest possible material. But they were sold by the million, all over the world. They can be found with every conceivable name – the Destroyer, the Terrible, the Titanic – and marked in various languages to suggest American, French or Belgian origin; they can be found with the proof marks of every country, plus a few that mean precisely nothing, none of which signify very much. The Eibar automatic is a study in itself; and yet, for all

The Colt M1911A1 was the standard US Army handgun in two world wars and was ideal for prisoner handling. Just after the Normandy landings US Military Police bring in some of the first German prisoners at the end of a Colt .45

that were sold, the genuine Browning still kept Fabrique National busy, and has done ever since.

After John Browning had passed his patents across to Fabrique National, he sat down to design a locked-breech pistol and this design was taken up by Colt in America. Browning's locking system has become known as the swinging-link, and in its first application it involved carrying the barrel on two hinged links attached at the muzzle and at the breech and pinned to the pistol frame beneath. The top surface of the barrel had transverse ribs cut in it, and these mated with transverse grooves cut into the undersurface of the top of the enveloping slide. A return spring beneath the

barrel kept the slide pressed forward, so that the breech-block section of the slide forced a cartridge from the butt-mounted magazine and into the chamber and then, because of the forward thrust, forced the entire barrel to move forward about the hinged links. This forward movement, thanks to the links, also lifted the barrel so that the transverse ribs locked into the slide when the breech was fully closed. Any rearward movement of the slide would now, because of the locking ribs, cause the barrel to move back as well, locked to the slide. Therefore the breech was firmly locked when the pistol fired and for a short time afterwards; as the slide moved back so the barrel hinged down until, eventually,

The Colt .45 M1911

the lugs disengaged and the barrel stopped moving, leaving the slide free to recoil and extract the fired case.

The first Colt automatic using this system was the Model 1900, of which about 3500 were made. It was chambered for a new .38 rimless cartridge and about 250 were bought by the US Army and Navy for trials. It was, by later standards, pretty crude but it taught both Colt and the military a lot about what was desirable and what was not. One bad feature was the firing pin, which was so long that when the external hammer was down, the tip of the pin rested on the cap of the chambered cartridge, a dangerous state of affairs. The next model to appear, the M1902 Sporting, shortened the firing pin into the inertia type, so that only a blow from the hammer could drive it forward with sufficient energy to protrude through the front of the breech block and fire the cartridge. Accompanying this model was the M1902 Military, a little larger and heavier and carrying eight shots in the magazine instead of seven. It also added a holding-open catch which held the slide back after the last shot had been fired, indicating the state of the gun to the firer. This was a very sound design and was to remain in production until 1929, but although the military were interested, they did not adopt it.

The military, in fact, were unlikely to adopt any weapon not of .45 calibre. The Spanish-American War and the Philippines insurrection had demonstrated that the .38 Special revolver cartridge was of little use in knocking down fanatic attackers, and in 1904 the US War Department set up a board of enquiry consisting of Col John T Thompson (who later developed the Thompson submachine-gun) and Col L A LaGarde. These two officers took a selection of weapons, including 7.65-mm and 9-mm Parabellum pistols, .38 and .45 Colt revolvers, and .38 Colt automatics, and proceeded to fire them into corpses, beef cattle and horses. The result of this gruesome exercise was to confirm that nothing less than a .45 bullet could be relied on in combat, and, accordingly, the War Department let it be known that only weapons firing a .45 bullet would be considered for test in future.

Colt therefore began by designing a new .45 cartridge for an automatic pistol, and then enlarged their pistol to suit. They were so confident that the design was a winner that they prepared production lines, but although the Army bought 200 for tests, no official adoption followed. The Model 1905 went on commercial sale and about 6000 were sold in the next six years; some of them had the butts slotted to take a wooden stock, in similar manner to the Mauser.

Though the Army didn't take to the Colt design – one objection was the absence of any safety device – it was good enough to make them realise that there did, at last, seem to be a possible alternative to the revolver, and on 28 December 1906 the Chief of Staff ordered a board of enquiry to be assembled at Springfield Arsenal, to carry out tests to decide on the Army's future handgun. The Chief of Ordnance had already advertised the forthcoming trial, specifying that only weapons of .45 calibre or over would be considered.

On 15 January 1907, the board looked at the submitted pistols. These were the Colt, Parabellum, Savage, Knoble, Bergmann and White-Merrill automatic pistols, the Colt and Smith & Wesson revolvers and the Webley-Fosbery automatic revolver. The Colt was a slightly improved model of the 1905; the Parabellum was of the same general design as the 7.65-mm model but had been hand-made in .45 calibre;

COLT .45 M1911

The US Army's standard pistol from 1911 to the present day; the best combat automatic pistol ever developed; and probably the first military weapon to become a centenarian, since there seems little likelihood of the American Army ever abandoning it for anything else. This sectioned drawing shows the system of locking designed by John Browning, in which lugs on top of the barrel engage in recesses in the slide and are withdrawn by the hinged link below the chamber as the gun is fired

Weight:	2 lb 7½ oz
Muzzle velocity:	1186 fps
Magazine:	7 shots

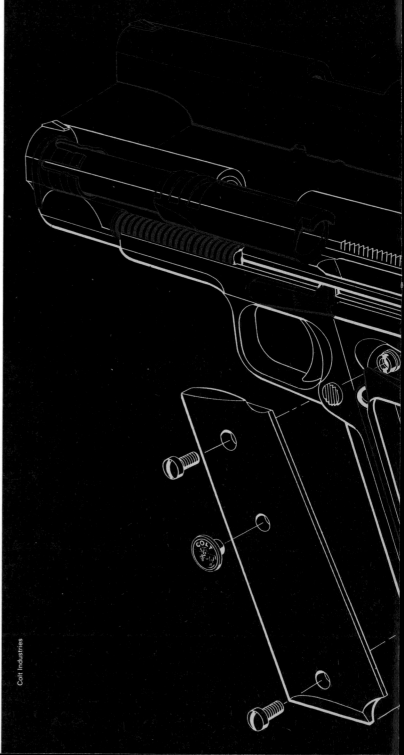

Colt Industries

A US government
agent, A 'fed' of the
1920s, proudly shows
off his Colt .45

American History Picture Library

BERGMANN-BAYARD 9-mm MODEL 1910

This pistol was designed by Theodor Bergmann, who managed to sell it to the Spanish Army. Due to business difficulties he was unable to manufacture it and gave the contract and licence to the Pieper company of Liège in Belgium. Their trademark was 'Bayard', from which comes the name. It is a locked breech pistol firing a powerful cartridge somewhat larger than the usual 9-mm Parabellum. It was later adopted by the Danish Army and by the Greeks

SIMPLEX 8-mm

The Simplex 8-mm pistol was actually a Bergmann design made in Belgium. It was marketed in England by the Wilkinson Sword Company in 1904–6

Weight:	1 lb 6 oz
Muzzle velocity:	790 fps
Magazine:	6 shots

the Savage and the other designs we can ignore for the moment.

The tests were exhaustive and the board finally reported in May 1907. In their view the Colt and Savage pistols were of sufficient merit to warrant buying 200 of each to issue them to cavalry troops for an extended field trial; the Parabellum was favourably noticed but was 'not recommended for a service test because its certainty of action . . . is not considered satisfactory . . .' However, Savage were unwilling to accept an order for only 200, so an attempt was made to obtain 200 Parabellum .45 models. But this fell through as DWM were not willing to make such a small number; it seems probable that they had their hands full with the incipient Germany Army order and were unwilling to speculate on the Americans adopting the pistol. Savage did, eventually, agree to produce the 200 pistols, Colt did likewise, and the field trials were carried out.

These showed that neither pistol was fully satisfactory but that the Colt held out the greatest promise, and the Army requested some minor modifications. By this time, too, the Ordnance Department had redesigned the .45 cartridge to take a 230-grain bullet (instead of the original 200-grain) which has remained the US standard ever since. Colt made the necessary modifications, and in 1911 the Colt .45 automatic pistol was officially adopted.

The principal changes from the earlier design made the weapon simpler, more reliable and safer. The major change was in the method of mounting the barrel. Instead of the two links, muzzle and breech, only one was now used, pinned beneath the breech. The muzzle was held in alignment by a bushing in the front of the slide; during recoil this bushing slid back along the barrel and was given sufficient clearance to permit the slight tilting of the barrel as the swinging link pulled down the breech and disengaged the locking lugs. Safety was attended to by fitting a manual safety catch on the frame, a grip safety device on the back of the butt, and a half-cock notch on the hammer. A seven-shot magazine fitted in the butt, and an eighth round could be loaded into the chamber over a full magazine. Experience was to prove the soundness of the design, and except for minor modifications – which were more cosmetic than functional – after the First World War, it has hardly changed since its introduction.

After thus galloping into 1911 with the Colt, we must now go back to see what else had appeared in that period, and we might start by looking at Britain. There the heavy revolver was the accepted military sidearm, and although the Army had tried the Parabellum they were quite unconvinced of its utility as a combat pistol. Power was what was needed; and to provide power and yet move into the automatic age, Col G V Fosbery, VC, came up with his automatic revolver. His first design was based on the well-tried Colt Frontier .45; the weapon was cut to pieces and reassembled so that barrel and cylinder were in a separate unit which could slide across the top of the butt frame, in much the same manner as the barrel and extension of the Mauser or Parabellum. The cylinder was incised with zig-zag grooves and straight cuts on its outer surface, which mated with a pin fixed to the top of the frame. As a result, when the cylinder unit slid back and forth over the frame, the pin, riding in these grooves, caused the cylinder to revolve; it first turned one-twelfth of a turn as the pistol recoiled, and then, as the return spring drove the barrel and

Weight: 2 lb 4 oz

Muzzle velocity: 1300 fps

Magazine: 6 or 10 shots

WEBLEY-FOSBERY .455 AUTOMATIC REVOLVER

Several people tried to make automatic revolvers but Fosbery was the only man to make a success of the idea. It was turned into a practical weapon by Webley & Scott, and the result was sold from 1901 until the end of the First World War. Although never adopted as a service arm it was used by hundreds of British officers during the war, but it was not a good design for withstanding the dirt of the trenches. As a target weapon it was excellent and many owners were handicapped in competitions since it was felt that they had an unfair advantage. It was also made in an 8-shot .38 version, though these are much less common

Weight: 2 lb 10 oz

Muzzle velocity: 770 fps

Cylinder: 6 shots

cylinder back again, the cylinder made another one-twelfth turn, so bringing the next chamber into alignment with the hammer, which had been cocked on the backward stroke. So that immediately after firing, the pistol was recocked, with a loaded chamber under the hammer.

Fosbery patented this idea in 1895, and the next year he took out a fresh patent in which the design was based on a Webley hinged-frame revolver, though in other respects the principle remained much the same. He then took the idea to Webley and they developed it into a viable weapon, putting it on sale in 1901. This, in .455 calibre, was the weapon tested by the US board in 1907. It was also produced in .38 Auto cartridge chambering, with an eight-shot cylinder.

The Webley-Fosbery was highly successful, being popular with target shooters for its 'soft' recoil; indeed, in many contests, Webley-Fosbery owners were officially handicapped as it was felt that they had an unfair advantage over competitors with conventional revolvers. But for all that the Army refused to accept it, though there was no bar to officers buying it as a personal weapon. An officer could carry what weapon he liked, provided it fired service ammunition; it was, the War Office reasoned, his neck, and he was entitled to protect it in the manner he preferred. But (to go forward a few years) the Webley-Fosbery met its match in the mud and dirt of Flanders during the First World War, when its multiplicity of sliding surfaces jammed with the filth of the trenches all too readily.

So if the Webley-Fosbery were not to the military's liking, there was still room for an automatic pistol, and in 1898 a Mr Hugh Gabbet-Fairfax appeared with a design of pistol which he offered to Webley. Gabbet-Fairfax was an indefatigable designer of all sorts of firearms, but his pistol, which eventually appeared on the market as the Mars, stands as his monument. Until recently it was the most powerful handgun ever produced, and it will probably stand for all time as the most complex.

The Mars worked on the long-recoil principle, and it was chambered, in a variety of calibres, for cartridges which Gabbet-Fairfax designed himself. As a contemporary report

put it 'he allowed his ideals to wander in the direction of high ballistics, and his pistols accordingly took on the form of young cannon.' The pistol was heavy, with a deep slab-sided frame which concealed a lot of machinery; a long fixed-spring casing extending under the barrel; and a barrel and rotating breech-block which slide across the top of the frame in front of an extremely large external hammer. A magazine was inserted into the butt in conventional manner; but the magazine was far from conventional in that its top carried a steel finger which extended up the front and over the top of the top cartridge, so that the cartridge could be removed only by pulling it out backwards.

On firing, the hammer fell on to a firing pin in the breech-block and the pistol fired. The barrel and breechblock, locked together, then recoiled for about 2 in across the top of the frame, cocking the hammer. At the end of the recoil stroke, the breechblock was rotated and unlocked, and held at the back of the frame. The barrel was then returned to the forward position, allowing the extractor in the breechblock to pull the empty cartridge case out of the chamber. As the barrel reached its forward position, a mechanical ejector was punched up to knock the empty case out of the feedway. During the recoil stroke a cartridge lifter had pulled a cartridge out of the magazine, and now, as the ejector finished its work, this unit lifted the fresh cartridge and held it up in the feedway. All this, of course, happened in the split second after the shot had been fired and while the firer was still holding the trigger pressed after the shot. He now relaxed his grip on the trigger, and this allowed the breechblock to run forward, chamber the round on the lifter, and lock into the breech opening. The lifter went down and hooked on to the next cartridge in the magazine and the pistol was ready to fire the next round.

The Mars appeared in 8.5-mm, 9-mm and .45-in calibres; the 9-mm fired a 156-grain bullet at 1650 ft a second, the .45 a 220-grain bullet at 1200 ft a second, while the 8.5-mm belted out a 139-grain bullet at 1750 ft a second to deliver a punch of 950 ft-lb at the muzzle. These were powerful cartridges, and the result on the firer was formidable; one

WEBLEY MARS 9-mm

The Mars automatic pistol, showing the bolt held at the rear of the frame, while the barrel has returned to the firing position. The cartridge lifter holds the next round ready for loading. When the trigger is released, the bolt will close, leaving the hammer cocked

Weight: 2 lb 11 oz

Muzzle velocity: 1200 fps

Magazine: 8 shots

Imperial War Museum

Sq Cdr CR Samson, the famous naval aviator of the First World War, seen here armed with a Webley automatic – standard Royal Naval Air Service issue

wrote afterwards that the pistol jumped wildly at every shot, finishing up pointing straight upwards somewhere over the firer's shoulder, and that if the firer had not had his finger hooked firmly into the trigger guard, he would probably have lost the pistol over his shoulder. Webley were not interested in developing the design under their own name, but made some pistols for Gabbet-Fairfax to sell, finance being arranged by the Mars Automatic Pistol Syndicate. The pistols were submitted for trial by the War Office and the Royal Navy, but they were not accepted for service. Since the designer had gambled on service acceptance, this spelt an end to his venture; he went bankrupt in 1903 and although there was an attempt to revive the design in the next year, it came to nothing. No more than about 70 Mars pistols were made. The epitaph of the design was to be found in the summary of trials carried out by the Royal Navy: 'Nobody who fired this pistol wished to fire it a second time.'

Abortive as the Mars proved to be, it at least had the effect of turning Webley's eyes inwards to their own design department. Mr W J Whiting, their principal designer, had done a great deal of work on Gabbet-Fairfax's design to turn it into a workable pistol, and he then, with the Mars as a glaring example of how not to do things, designed a new weapon to be marketed under the Webley name. In 1903 a prototype appeared, chambered for the regulation .455 revolver cartridge; the pistol operated on short recoil principles, the breechblock being locked to the barrel by two arms, one at each side of the breech. As the barrel and breech recoiled across the frame, so a hump on the frame caused the arms to lift and disengage from the barrel. The barrel stopped, while the breechblock ran back, cocked an external hammer, and then ran forward, chambering a cartridge from the butt-mounted magazine. As the breech closed, the barrel and block moved forward and the lumps on the frame cammed the locking arms back into place.

This 1903 model was not very successful and Whiting produced a fresh design the next year. This used a breech-block sliding in a deep-section frame, locked to the barrel by a vertically-moving locking bolt. It was still chambered for the rimmed .455 revolver cartridge, was an enormous and heavy pistol, and it sold in small numbers. The rimmed cartridge proving difficult to function in an automatic weapon, the next move was to produce a new semi-rimmed round specifically for automatic pistols, still in .455 calibre, after which the pistol design was modified to use the new round.

Whiting was still not satisfied that the best design had been reached, and in 1906 he patented a fresh model in which the barrel breech end was square-sectioned and carried two slanting ribs on each side, mating with two slanting grooves in the slide-cum-breechblock. The shape of the pistol frame ensured that the first movement of recoil kept the barrel level so that the interconnecting ribs and grooves locked barrel and breech together. After a short recoil travel, the barrel was allowed to drop slightly, which brought ribs and grooves out of engagement, so that the slide could then recoil independently, cocking the external hammer and reloading on the return stroke. As the breech closed, so the ribs and grooves lined up and the frame forced the barrel up to bring everything into engagement and lock the breech. One unusual feature was that the recoil spring was a large V-spring lying beneath the right-hand butt grip. One arm of this spring was held against a

*Royal Naval Air Service recruits
undergo small-arms training at
Crystal Palace in 1916 with
Webley automatics*

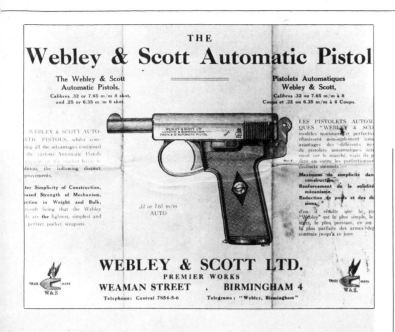

projection in the frame, while the tip of the other arm rode in a recess in the slide, so that as the slide recoiled, the spring was closed and compressed. Years of experience with revolvers and sporting guns had taught Webley a great deal about V-springs, and they were probably wise to adopt a design they knew rather than try to obtain a coil spring with the performance they wanted.

The 1906 design was a good one, and Webley produced it with minor variations and in different calibres for several years. In .455 calibre it was adopted by the Royal Navy in 1913 and in 9-mm Browning Long calibre by the South African Police in 1920. It was extremely reliable, but the carefully-machined barrel and slide made it expensive and heavy and, in most users' views, the butt was set too squarely to the barrel for accurate instinctive shooting.

While the heavy locked-breech military pistols were being developed, Whiting designed a smaller model with an un-locked breech. In appearance it resembled the military weapons, with the square slide and exposed barrel, but the barrel was solidly fixed to the frame and the slide operated by simple blow-back. This was produced in .25, .32 and .380 chambering for many years, and in 1911 the .32 model was adopted as the official pistol of the City of London and Metropolitan Police forces, as well as by several other police forces in England and Wales. This came about because of the Sidney Street Siege when a gang of criminals took refuge in a building in Sidney Street, London, and resisted arrest by

**WEBLEY & SCOTT .455
AUTOMATIC PISTOL MK I**

This pistol was adopted by the Royal Navy in 1915 in .455 calibre and similar models were sold commercially in 9-mm and .38 Super Auto calibres. A very robust weapon, it has a square-set grip which makes instinctive shooting difficult. Smaller versions in .32 calibre were the standard police pistol in Britain for many years, and licensed copies were manufactured in the USA by Harrington & Richardson. The .455 model

was fitted with a wooden butt and issued to the Royal Horse Artillery in 1915 and was also widely used by the early Royal Flying Corps observers and pilots

Weight:	2 lb 8 oz
Muzzle velocity:	750 fps
Magazine:	7 shots

opening fire with automatic pistols. Three policemen were killed, and eventually a squad of Scots Guards had to be called up to shoot their way into the building. The subsequent enquiry recommended the adoption of automatic pistols by police forces and the Webley & Scott automatic was chosen.

The 1907 US Army trial had featured a Savage pistol, a pistol which did so well that a further 200 were bought for extended trials. The Savage was one of the relatively small groups of pistols which adopted a system of breech locking which depended on the barrel's being able to rotate. Two other pistols using the same basic system, though differing in detail, were the Roth-Steyr of 1908 and the Steyr of 1912, both produced in Austro-Hungary. The Steyr designs (both by Karl Krnka and Georg Roth) were fairly straightforward and serve as a good introduction to the idea. The pistol barrel was made with lugs protruding from its surface, some straight, some laid in helical fashion. The slide of the pistol was furnished with a right-angled groove to engage in a top lug on the barrel, while the frame of the pistol had grooving which engaged firstly with a bottom square lug and secondly with the helical lug. When the pistol was fired, the slide attempted to move back, being forced by the pressure in the cartridge case, but move-

ment was prevented by the top barrel lug being engaged in the slide groove. Consequently, both the barrel and the slide began to move back, and as this movement took place, so the helical lug on the barrel was forced through its corresponding groove in the frame. This caused the barrel to rotate through 90°, and at the end of that movement the square lug under the barrel came into a frame groove so as to halt the barrel, while the lug on top of the barrel had moved out of the groove in the slide and into a longitudinal cut-away, so that the slide was now free to recoil on its own.

It was a very elegant system, demanding precise machining, but the Steyr 1912 pistol was one of the best service pistols ever built; the only thing that spoiled its chances was the fact that Steyr, for their own good reasons, chose to chamber it for a cartridge in 9-mm calibre of their own devising, which did not fit any other weapon. Had it been produced for something more popular, there is every chance it might have been more successful.

The Savage pistol worked along similar lines, but the rotation of the barrel was no more than 5°, so that the unlocking was completed very rapidly indeed. Much ink has been spilt on this subject over the years, and it seems, on

STEYR 9-mm MODEL 1912

This Austrian service pistol used the same rotating barrel system of breech locking as the earlier Roth-Steyr, but used a slide configuration instead of a separate breech bolt. Loading was still done by pulling back the slide and inserting a charger, then sweeping the cartridges into the fixed magazine in the butt. The cartridge was the 9-mm Steyr, a longer and more powerful round than the 9-mm Parabellum. During the Second World War many of these pistols, still in use

by the Austrian Army, were converted to fire the 9-mm Parabellum cartridge, since this was more easily obtained. It was an excellent weapon, and had it been chambered for the more popular cartridge in the first place it might well have become more widely used

Weight:	2 lb 3 oz
Muzzle velocity:	1100 fps
Magazine:	8 shots

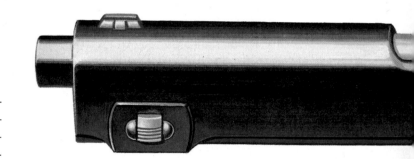

ROTH-STEYR 8-mm M1908

Adopted by the Austro-Hungarian Army in 1908, this pistol was an unusual design, by Karel Krnka and Georg Roth of Vienna. The barrel and bolt were locked together on firing and after a short recoil the barrel was rotated by cams to release the bolt lugs and allow the bolt to recoil. Like almost all of Krnka's designs it was loaded by opening the bolt and placing a charger of cartridges into the bolt-way, then pushing the cartridges into the butt with the thumb. The striker was cocked by pulling the trigger; this, it was said, was to prevent a cocked pistol being fired inadvertently if the cavalryman's horse suddenly reared up

Weight:	2 lb 4 oz
Muzzle velocity:	1045 fps
Magazine:	10 shots

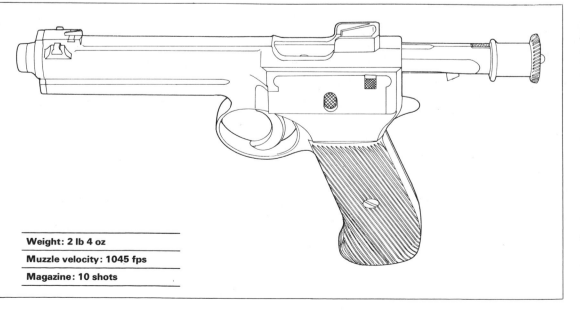

US Army officers testing automatics just before the United States came into the First World War

balance, more charitable to say that the Savage system was a delayed blow-back rather than a fully-locked breech. Searle, the designer, made some claims to the effect that the torque of the bullet passing up the rifling helped to delay the rotation of the barrel and thus ensured that it remained locked until the bullet had left; but this is a dubious argument. It can equally well be claimed that the axial pressure of the bullet in the rifling would tend to turn the barrel that much more quickly. What is certain is that a German experiment, some years later, showed with the aid of high-speed spark photography that the breech of the Savage .32 pistol actually opened somewhat more quickly than that of a plain blow-back Browning pistol of the same calibre.

In any event, the Savage did not achieve military success in 1907, but a smaller version, in .32 calibre, was put on the civil market soon afterwards and was available until the middle 1920s. It did, eventually, become a military pistol, though hardly in the way that the company had envisaged. In the First World War the Portuguese Army were unable to obtain supplies of the Parabellum, their usual military pistol, from Germany and instead of going across the border and buying in Spain, they bought up supplies in the US.

SAVAGE .32 MODEL 1907

The Savage pistol used a rotating barrel to hold the slide locked during firing, but since the rotation was no more than 5°, it did not stay locked for very long, and really should be considered a 'delayed blow-back' weapon. A .45 version was tested by the US Army in 1907 and was very successful, but after extensive trials was beaten by the Colt M1911 for official adoption. The Savage company then sold the pistol on the civil market for many years. It was taken as a military weapon by the Portuguese Army during the First World War and is still relatively common in that country

Weight: 1 lb 5 oz

Muzzle velocity: 950 fps

Magazine: 10 shots

REVOLVERS KEEP PACE

During the time that the automatic pistol had been making its first tentative steps, the revolver had not been standing still. The most significant step was taken by Colt in the 1880s; at that time their line of solid-frame gate-loaded revolvers appeared out of date by comparison with the hinged-frame, simultaneous-ejection models being put out by Smith & Wesson, and they began to examine methods of more efficient ejection which would not bring them into patent litigation. In 1881 William Mason, Colt factory manager, had patented a revolver design in which the cylinder could swing out of the solid frame in a sideways arc, a cam device automatically forcing out an ejecting plate at the end of the stroke. This turned out to be too delicate to be practical, but Mason made improvements and in 1889 Colt put their New Navy revolver on the market and introduced the side-swinging cylinder design to the public. In this model the cylinder was carried on a 'crane' and locked by a latch which entered the cylinder axis from the standing breech and was operated by pulling back on a thumb-catch on the left side of the frame. A hand ejecting rod lay in front of the cylinder, under the barrel when the gun was in the firing mode, and, with the cylinder swung out, pressure on this rod forced out the usual star-shaped ejecting plate and cleared the cylinder.

The US Navy bought 5000 of these pistols in .38 calibre, and, according to legend, it was the Navy's 'experts' who were responsible for the fact that the cylinder rotated anti-clockwise, opposite to the direction of any previous Colt design. Whatever the reason may have been, the result was that the pawl which thrust up on the ratchet to rotate the cylinder also had the effect of pushing the cylinder outwards, in the direction of opening, and thus, after a little wear there was a constant misalignment of chamber and barrel, resulting in minute shavings of lead being removed from the bullet as it passed from one to the other.

Several other revolvers on similar lines to the New Navy were made and sold by Colt in the next few years, including New Army and Marine Corps models, but one or two defects had to be corrected. One serious problem was that it was possible to operate the double-action lock while the cylinder was still part way out of the frame and not properly locked. It might be just short of the locked position, and with a fraction of the cartridge cap in line with the hammer; and if fired in this condition, a serious accident could ensue. Colt cured this by placing a slot in the rear of the crane hinge pin, into which a portion of the firing mechanism moved when the hammer was operated. Unless this slot was correctly aligned by having the cylinder properly closed and locked, then the hammer could not move and the gun was incapable of firing.

Even if the US Army and Navy were happy with the design, Colt were not; the counter-clockwise cylinder rotation irritated them, the lockwork was too fragile and repair was difficult. In 1893, therefore, the company introduced a New Pocket model for commercial sale which reverted to the clockwise cylinder rotation and introduced a totally new design of trigger and hammer mechanism, a great deal more robust than the pattern used on the military models. The New Pocket appeared first in .32 calibre, and in 1897 came the New Service, a heavy model using the same basic mechanism but chambered for the heaviest loadings, such as .45 Colt, .455 Eley and .44 Russian.

In 1905 Colt made their last major step in revolver design by introducing their Positive Safety Lock, including the word Positive in their nomenclature to make sure that the advantage was recognised, so that the New Pocket became the Pocket Positive and the New Police now became the Police Positive.

The Positive Lock was developed to overcome a basic defect in revolver lock designs; the fact that if, during thumb-cocking, the hammer were to be accidentally released, or if the pistol were dropped on to a hard surface and struck on the hammer, then there was every chance that the hammer would be driven forward sufficiently hard to fire the cartridge beneath the hammer. The lock took the form of a small steel arm inside the frame which was linked to the trigger and hammer mechanism. When the mechanism was at rest, this arm reached up in front of the hammer and physically blocked the hammer from reaching far enough forward for the firing pin to touch the cartridge cap. Only when the trigger was pressed back was this arm withdrawn; merely thumbing back the hammer did not affect the movement of the arm, so that if the thumb slipped and the hammer went down, the Positive Safety Lock stood in the way and prevented an accident. Only pulling the trigger, in the conscious act of firing, would remove the intercepting arm and allow the hammer to fire the pistol.

Colt were not the pioneers of this sort of safety device. The Iver Johnson Company, who made a variety of less expensive revolvers for home defence had adopted their Hammer the Hammer safety device in 1897. This took away the firing pin from the hammer face, where it had been ever since the cartridge revolver had been born, and placed a separate firing pin inside the standing breech, causing it to be struck by the flat-faced hammer. But the face of the hammer was formed so that it actually struck solidly against the pistol frame without reaching the firing pin; attached to the trigger mechanism was a transfer bar which, when the trigger was properly pulled, was forced upwards to sit behind the firing pin. Then, as the hammer dropped, its face struck the transfer bar and the blow was passed on to the firing pin. It was an eminently simple and effective design, and, the patents having long expired, it was widely adopted in the US after the enactment of the Gun Control Act, 1968, made revolver safety devices mandatory.

Smith & Wesson appear not to have been unduly put out by the appearance of the New Navy and subsequent Colt models with the side-opening cylinder, and continued to make their hinged-frame pistols for several years more. But in 1887 they produced something of a novelty with their New Departure or Safety Hammerless revolver, which became known to the public at large as the Lemon Squeezer. The novelty lay in the adoption of a hammerless outline, and the incorporation of a safety grip in the butt. The pistol was, in strict fact, a hinged-frame revolver with a normal sort of hammer, but the hammer had its cocking spur removed and it was entirely concealed in the rise of the frame behind the cylinder. This meant that it could be carried in the pocket and withdrawn rapidly without the danger of the hammer catching in the clothing; indeed, as some people discovered, it could even be fired from inside the pocket, something difficult to do with an ordinary hammer-type revolver. The safety grip was a spring-loaded rib running down the back-strap of the pistol butt and linked to the trigger and hammer mechanism in such a way that unless the grip was held

FIRST IN
THE FIGHT~
ALWAYS
FAITHFUL~
BE A U.S. MARINE!

JAMES MONTGOMERY FLAGG

This US Marine recruiting poster of 1917 speaks for itself. The weapon is a Marine Corps Model Colt revolver

properly and the safety latch forced in, the hammer would not rise and the weapon could not be fired. It was this raised safety latch which led to the Lemon Squeezer nickname. The weapon became so popular that it was to stay in production until 1940.

With the success of the New Departure model, Smith & Wesson could safely ignore the side-opening cylinder for a few years, until in 1896 they produced the .32 Hand Ejector which marked their entry into the side-opening field. By this time it appears that Mason's original patent had expired, and Smith & Wesson were able to evade other provisions of Colt's patented designs by simply reversing the movement of the latch which locked the cylinder into place, requiring it to be pushed forward instead of pulled back. Various revolvers of this pattern were produced in subsequent years, including about 3000 bought by the US Army during the Spanish-American War. The design subsequently crystallised into the Military and Police model, which has been in production, in one modification or another, ever since.

One minor defect of the Smith & Wesson design was the lack of rigidity because of latching the cylinder only at its rear end, and in 1902 D B Wesson took out patents for a much improved system of locking. The cylinder axis and the hand ejector rod now carried a central locking-pin throughout their whole length, and a lug was forged on the barrel into which the front end of the ejecting rod closed. Inside the lug was a spring-loaded pin which snapped in place into the hollow end of the ejecting rod and so locked the front end of the assembly; at the same time, this pin forced the central locking rod back, assisted by a spring, so that the rear end went into a recess in the standing breech and thus locked the rear end of the assembly. Pushing the release catch forced in the locking rod to disconnect at the rear end and also to force in the pin in the barrel lug and unlock the front end. This gave a very solid lock, and the under-barrel lug has been a feature of Smith & Wesson revolvers ever since.

In 1906 came the Smith & Wesson equivalent of the Colt Positive Lock, a component called a rebound slide inside the lockwork which, unless drawn back by the trigger, fouled the bottom of the hammer and prevented it from falling on to the chambered cartridge. Finally, in 1907, came the Triple Lock or New Century revolvers, probably the finest revolvers ever made; in these, the cylinder locking was improved by the addition of a third locking lug which firmly anchored the crane arm into the frame just in front of the cylinder, thus making the whole cylinder unit as rigid as it could possibly be. This design brought about a small change in the appearance of the pistols, since the simple barrel lug for the front end of the ejecting rod was replaced by a long shroud which completely held the entire length of the ejecting rod beneath the barrel, as well as acting to lock the forward end. The only drawback with this design was the amount of careful machining and fitting it demanded, and, as was found during the First World War, the fact that the slightest amount of dirt in the locking surfaces was enough to prevent the revolver being closed or opened.

With the Colt New Service, the Smith & Wesson New Century and the later Webley models, revolver design had just about reached its peak. But there were still some inventors who felt that things could be improved. And one of the areas of possible improvement lay in the basic construction of a revolver. The fundamental feature of the revolver is that you

SMITH & WESSON .45 M1917

As with Colt, so with Smith & Wesson; this was their commercial .45 Hand Ejector model adapted to the use of the service .45 auto cartridge. But in this case it was possible to fire the cartridge without the use of the 'half-moon clip', since Smith & Wesson always machined a step in their chambers on which the mouth of the cartridge case rested. Nevertheless, you still had to use the clip, otherwise the rimless cases wouldn't eject. After the war, when many of these revolvers (and the Colt) were sold off to the civil market, one ammunition maker found it profitable to make a .45 cartridge with an extra-thick rim to take up the excess space behind the cylinder and function without the clips

Weight:	2 lb 4 oz
Muzzle velocity:	860 fps
Cylinder:	6 shots

Keystone

Italian partisans some armed with 1889 vintage Bodeo service revolvers, gather round a Daimler scout car in the square of a northern Italian town in late 1944

COLT .45 M1917

When America entered the First World War, it needed pistols in a hurry for the sudden increase in soldiers; the standard .45 automatic could not be made quickly enough, and the Army therefore bought revolvers. But they had to fire the same .45 rimless cartridge as the automatic pistol. This was done by making 'half-moon clips' to hold three cartridges; two would drop into the cylinder and the extractor could then use the clip to eject the empty cases after firing, a thing which would not be possible with rimless cartridges and no clip. Use of the clip meant a larger gap at the rear of the cylinder, but otherwise this is the commercial New Service model which had been introduced in 1897. Large numbers were held in reserve and were issued once more in 1941

Weight: 2 lb 8 oz
Muzzle velocity: 860 fps
Cylinder: 6 shots

FRENCH 8-mm MODÈLE D'ORDONNANCE MLE 1892

The Mle 1892 was the first revolver in a major army to move away from the heavy 11-mm .45 calibre range, and the reason was partly economic; the Mle 1886 service rifle was 8-mm calibre, and adopting the same calibre for the revolver meant a saving in barrel-making machinery. Unfortunately it meant taking a calibre which was really too small for combat use, but the French accepted this and the Mle 1892 served valiantly until the 1950s. One unusual feature is that the cylinder swings out to the right for re-loading; every other revolver with a side-swinging cylinder swings it out to the left, which seems more logical for a right-handed shooter. They order things differently in France

Weight: 1 lb 14 oz
Muzzle velocity: 750 fps
Cylinder: 6 shots

have a cylinder, containing the cartridges, behind the barrel. So that the cylinder can revolve freely, there must be some degree of space between the cylinder face and the rear end of the barrel; therefore when the cartridge is fired, the bullet passes across this gap and, inevitably, some of the propelling gas must leak out of the gap, reducing the power available to push the bullet. Moreover, when the revolver gets a little worn, there will be a slight misalignment between cylinder and barrel and the bullet will be 'shaved' as it passes the gap, resulting in an out-of-balance and inaccurate bullet.

Attempts had been made to overcome this problem in the earliest days of revolvers, as, for example, when Collier patented an idea for sliding the cylinder forward to force the chamber mouth over the rear end of the barrel, but the idea had lapsed for many years. Then, in 1886, a Belgian designer named Pieper patented a system for cartridge arms in which the essential point was that the cartridge case was to have an extended mouth and, by either moving the cylinder forward, or moving the barrel back, or by actually pushing the cartridge forward in its chamber, the front end of the cartridge case was to be made to enter the rear of the barrel and seal the gap. Pieper made a small number of light rifles on this principle, in which an under-lever (reminiscent of the Winchester carbine) pulled the barrel back into a tight fit in the mouth of the chamber and enclosed the mouth of the cartridge. He later followed this with a design of revolver in 1890, specimens of which were later made by the Austrian Arms Company as their M1892 model. But for some unaccountable reason Pieper allowed the all-important patent to lapse, with the result that another Belgian gunsmith, Leon Nagant, appeared in 1892 with a design of gas-seal revolver which was little more than a slight modification of Pieper's design.

Whether Nagant was a better gunsmith than Pieper is open to doubt, but there can be no argument that he was a better salesman, for he was the only man ever to make a success of a gas-seal design. The Nagant M1892 revolver was a solid-frame, seven-shot model, gate-loaded and with rod ejection. As the trigger was pressed (or the hammer cocked) so the cylinder was thrust forward so that the mouth of the topmost chamber enveloped the chamfered rear end of the barrel, and the mouth of the cartridge entered the barrel. At the same time an abutment or wedge block was thrust up behind the cylinder so that the force of recoil would not blow it away from the barrel when the pistol was fired, and finally the hammer was released to fire the cartridge. The cartridge itself was of a special design in which the bullet was entirely concealed inside the case, the case mouth extending a fraction of an inch past the bullet tip to form the necessary seal across the gap when cylinder and barrel came together.

Nagant had, some years before this, co-operated in designing a rifle for the Russian Imperial Army and, doubtless on the strength of the connections thus formed, he was able to sell this revolver design to the Russians who adopted it as their service pistol in 7.62-mm calibre in 1895. A single-action model was produced for the use of troops and a double-action model for officers. Nagant also manufactured similar revolvers for commercial sale, as well as making them for supply to Russia, but soon the Russians took over the manufacture, producing them in the Tula arsenal, and in 1901 they bought the patent rights from Nagant entirely. Nagant no longer made gas seal revolvers, but the Russians continued to manufacture them up to the Second World War.

Ever since Nagant made this pistol, there has been argument about whether or not the gas seal was of any practical value. Precise comparison is not possible, since there is no revolver of exactly comparable characteristics – barrel length, chambering etc – but of a non-gas-seal pattern with which a Nagant could be compared. Experiments performed over the years, however, suggest that the difference in velocity between a gas-seal and a non-sealing revolver might be about 50 ft/sec in muzzle velocity. The Russian M1895 fired a 108-grain bullet at 1000 ft/sec, giving a muzzle energy of 240 ft/lb. Reducing the velocity by 50 ft/sec brings the muzzle energy down to 216 ft/lb. Bearing in mind that the generally accepted figure for producing a casualty is 50 ft/lb of energy, it does seem that the complication outweighs the gain in efficiency.

NAGANT 7.62-mm M1895 REVOLVER

The Nagant gas-seal revolver was unique in military service. It was designed in Belgium and adopted by the Russian Army, who afterwards bought out the patents and manufactured it themselves. It stayed in use until the end of the Second World War. On pulling the trigger, or pulling back the hammer, the cylinder moved forward so that the end of the barrel entered the mouth of the chamber. A wedge came up behind the cylinder to support it against the recoil. The cartridge case had an extended mouth which totally enclosed the bullet and entered into the barrel so as to span the gap and thus seal against any possible leak of gas

Weight: 1 lb 12 oz

Muzzle velocity: 1000 fps

Cylinder: 7 shots

The Handgun Goes to War: 1914–18

When the armies of Europe went to war in 1914, they went with their issue Parabellums, Webleys, Steyrs and so forth, but the enormous wastage of every sort of munition soon led to the introduction of new designs, pistols which in the normal course of events would have never seen the inside of a military store. The standard French pistol, for example, was an 8-mm solid-frame revolver, the Modèle 1892, and when supplies of this ran out, the French Government turned to the Spanish gunmakers of Eibar as being the quickest source of supply. As it happened, the Eibar firm of Gabilondo y Urresti had, in 1914, introduced a 7.65-mm blow-back pistol, loosely copied from the Browning M1903 design, which carried nine rounds in the magazine, unusual at that time. This was called the Ruby, and the French Army, after a few tests, decided that it would fill their requirements. In May 1915 they contracted with Gabilondo to produce 10,000 pistols a month until further notice. In August they stepped this up to 30,000 a month and let it be known that anything over that figure would be received without comment.

As might be imagined, the production of 30,000 pistols a month by Gabilondo, who were only a small firm, was out of the question, and they sub-contracted the job to eight or nine other companies in the neighbourhood. Even this could not meet the French demand and a dozen or more small companies got into the act, turning out copies of the Ruby under their own names and supplying them to France, and later to Italy. It managed to see the French Army through the war, and it was the foundation of several gunmaking companies who continued to turn out the Ruby design under hundreds of different names until the Civil War.

The German Army also needed pistols, but their standard service Parabellum was generally available for front-line troops. To make up deficiencies they contracted with Mauser to make several thousand C/96 Military Model pistols in 9-mm Parabellum chambering, but for staff officers and those who did not have to have a heavy-calibre pistol, they bought large numbers of 7.65-mm blow-backs, notably the Beholla and the Langenhan. Both were slightly odd; the Beholla had its barrel held in place by a crosspin which had to be driven out of the frame though a tiny hole in the slide before the pistol could be dismantled for cleaning. The Langenhan had a separate breechblock held in place by a somewhat hazardous screw lock which tended to come unscrewed by vibration until it gave way completely and the breechblock shot out into the firer's face.

Another odd German weapon was the Artillery Parabellum pistol, a version of the Pistole '08 having an 8-in barrel, long-range sights, and a peculiar snail type of helical drum magazine which had an extended tongue to go into the pistol butt. This held 32 rounds and when the auxiliary wooden butt was clipped in place, the whole thing resembled a short carbine. It was reputedly issued to NCOs of artillery and machine-gun units for close defence, and it was used by crews of coastal motorboats. For some years it was believed that this pistol was first issued in 1917, but recent research has shown that it was authorised for issue as early as July 1913, though the snail magazine was not issued until 1917. One unlooked-for result of the adoption of the snail magazine was that the standard 9-mm ammunition would not feed evenly; at that time the bullet was conical in shape, with a flattened tip, and it was

A French **Voltigeur** *armed with a Chauchat light machine-gun and a Ruby pistol, presumably for self-defence when the notoriously unreliable Chauchat broke down*

GLISENTI 9-mm MODEL 1910

The Glisenti was adopted by the Italian Army in 1910 to replace the Bodeo revolver. The 9-mm Glisenti cartridge is to the same dimensions as the more common 9-mm Parabellum

Weight: 1 lb 13 oz	
Muzzle velocity: 1050 fps	
Magazine: 7 shots	

found necessary to develop a new one with a more conventional rounded nose. Since this was easier to make it gradually replaced the original (Luger-designed) bullet and has since become the world's standard in this calibre.

The Italian Army had adopted an automatic pistol in 1910, the 9-mm Glisenti; it was not a particularly good design. In general appearance it looked a little like the Parabellum, with a prominent barrel and well-raked grip, but the mechanism consisted of a bolt moving in the receiver and locked by a rather weak strut. It was in short supply, and in 1915 the Pietro Beretta company were asked to produce a pistol. This firm had been in the firearms business since 1680, producing shotguns, but they now turned to the pistol field with good effect. Their Model 1915 was a simple but robust blowback in 7.65-mm calibre which they followed by a 9-mm model chambered for the 9-mm Glisenti cartridge. This cartridge was an unfortunate mistake; it had exactly the same dimensions as the 9-mm Parabellum and used the same sort of conical bullet, but it had a weaker powder loading. It served well in the Glisenti and in the blowback Beretta, but the trouble was that since the 9-mm Parabellum cartridge fitted it, there was a great chance, especially in the confusion of war, that somebody would load them. This had a severe effect on both these pistols, though it generally stopped short of serious accidents.

When the United States entered the war, their troops were, of course, provided with the Colt M1911 .45 automatic; or at least, as many troops as there were pistols. The rest had to be given revolvers, and large numbers of Colt and Smith & Wesson late models – the New Service Colt and the Military Smith & Wesson – were issued as the Revolver M1917. To simplify ammunition supply, both were in .45 calibre and the cylinders were shortened so that .45 automatic pistol cartridges could be loaded. The auto pistol cartridges were, of course, rimless, and in the normal course of events they would not chamber satisfactorily; in the Colt pistols they dropped straight through the chamber, but the Smith & Wesson pistols had a slight step in the chamber which held the mouth of the case. Even so, there was nothing for the ejection plate to get hold of, and the cartridges had to be clipped, three at a time, into half-moon clips and then loaded into the chambers; it was this additional thickness of the half-moon clips that demanded that the cylinders be shorter than normal.

This Women's Auxiliary Naval Service officer, 1917-vintage, looks businesslike at the end of a .455 Webley

PARABELLUM PISTOLE, LANGE MODELL '08

The long barrelled version of the P'08 was introduced in 1913 and it could be used for volley fire up to distances of 600m (2000 ft) with the stock fitted to the pistol butt. The *Trommelmagazin* (snail magazine) patented in 1908 was issued as the TM 08 in 1917 and contained 32 rounds

Weight: 2 lb 7 oz

Muzzle velocity: 1230 fps

Magazine: 8/32 rounds

Revolutionaries in Berlin, 1919, armed with rifles and Mauser M/96s await the onslaught of the Freikorps

Imperial War Museum

Berliner Konzerthaus
Bunter Abend

BORN OUT OF WAR

In the 1920s most countries were more concerned with overhauling their machine-guns and weapons of that nature than with worrying about pistols, since, so far as the military were concerned, the pistols they had used appeared to be satisfactory. But the designers and manufacturers were less complacent, and before the smoke had cleared away they were busy. Foremost among them was John Browning; he had begun improving his 1911 Colt design just before the war but had dropped it to concentrate on machine-gun design. In the early 1920s, he took it up once more. It has been asserted that he produced the design in answer to a French Army request for a new pistol, but there is no evidence to support this, and the French Army have always shown a marked reluctance to go outside their own country in peacetime for weapon designs. In 1923 Browning filed for patent protection and then handed the designs over to the Fabrique National, of Liège, for their development engineers to turn his drawings and idea into a production item.

Browning's principal change was to the operation of his swinging-link locking system. While it was a simple and effective system, the link did tend to wear with use, and, in theory at any rate, there was a source of inaccuracy in that the barrel began moving slightly down before the bullet had left the muzzle. Sergeant Alvin York, US Army, who marched in 132 prisoners at the point of an M1911, having stopped a bayonet charge on a one-shot-one-man basis and despatched a Maxim gun squad on similar lines, had not heard about this inaccuracy, of course, which was perhaps just as well for him.

Nevertheless, Browning took out the swinging-link and replaced it with a solid lug forged as part of the barrel, into which a shaped cam-path was cut. This path engaged with a crosspin in the pistol frame, and when the pistol recoiled, the pin acted on the cam to allow a degree of axial recoil and then pull the barrel down, out of engagement with the slide. The net result was the same, but there was a finite axial movement which improved accuracy and the solid forged lug was less likely to wear. Another advantage of the new design was that the pistol was to be chambered for the 9-mm Parabellum cartridge and the butt magazine would hold no fewer than 13 rounds. As a slight counter to this, the thicker butt meant a redesign of the trigger operating mechanism which resulted in a slightly less 'target-shooting oriented' trigger pull, but since this was to be a combat weapon, the FN engineers did not worry unduly about that.

Browning died in 1926, the patents being granted in 1927, and by 1928 the Browning Pistolet Grand Puissance (High Power) was completed. The intention was to market it in 1929, but the bottom fell out of the stock market, the world entered the depression years, and the FN management deferred production. Things began to look better in 1934 and production began, the pistol now being called the Model 35. The Belgian Army adopted it at once, and Estonia, Lithuania, China and Peru were immediately in the queue for supplies. It was, and still is, an outstanding weapon.

Across the other side of Europe, another pistol using Browning's swinging-link design appeared, the Soviet Army's Tokarev TT30. The Soviets had decided to replace the ageing Nagant revolver, and Fedor Tokarev, an outstanding designer, produced a modification of the Browning design. The overall slide and swinging link were the same, but Tokarev instituted two notable refinements; firstly, the hammer and lockwork

Chinese Nationalists (one officer is a woman) delightedly examine a Browning M1922

NAMBU 8-mm PISTOL

Colonel Nambu first showed his automatic pistol in 1909, and although Japanese officers were permitted to use it, it was not adopted officially until 1915, the Fourth Year of the Taisho Era, which gives rise to the name. The mechanism is very similar to that of the Glisenti, using a wedge to lock the breech bolt, and the recoil spring is set off to one side, in its own tunnel in the frame. The only safety device is a grip safety on the front of the butt. A smaller version in 7-mm calibre, called the Baby Nambu was produced for staff officers. A modified version of the Fourth Year was made in 1925, the Fourteenth Year Model; this had some minor changes and added a safety catch, but it was still recognisably Nambu

Weight: 1 lb 15 oz

Muzzle velocity: 1100 fps

Magazine: 8 shots

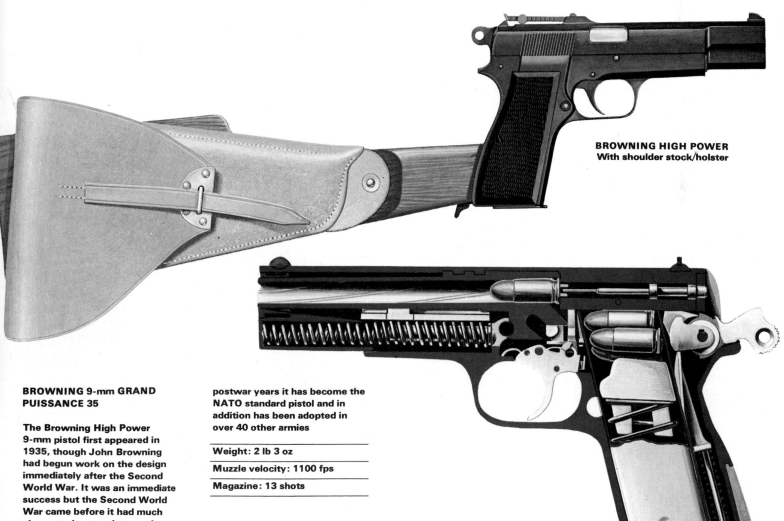

BROWNING HIGH POWER
With shoulder stock/holster

BROWNING 9-mm GRAND PUISSANCE 35

The Browning High Power 9-mm pistol first appeared in 1935, though John Browning had begun work on the design immediately after the Second World War. It was an immediate success but the Second World War came before it had much chance to become known. It was made in Canada for the Nationalist Chinese Army and for the Canadian and British Armies, and continued in production in Belgium for the benefit of the German Army. In postwar years it has become the NATO standard pistol and in addition has been adopted in over 40 other armies

Weight: 2 lb 3 oz

Muzzle velocity: 1100 fps

Magazine: 13 shots

A Russian officer leads a counter-attack waving his men on with a Tokarev pistol

were mounted in a removable unit so that they could be rapidly removed and cleaned or mended, always a difficult job on the Colt M1911. Secondly, he appreciated the fact that the weakest part of any automatic pistol lay in the magazine; this was usually a thin sheet-metal component, but the lips at the mouth were critical in their shape and angle to ensure reliable feeding. Yet these very lips were the most easily-damaged part of the whole pistol, and once the magazine was deformed, reliability went until a new one could be obtained. He therefore made the magazine lips a simple turnover shape which did no more than hold the cartridges in place, and actually machined the feed lips into the frame of the pistol. Now it mattered little if the magazine took a knock; provided it was roughly straightened so that the cartridges could pass through, reliable feed was assured by the hard steel lips.

Poland, Russia's neighbour, had become an independent nation in 1918 and, conscious of her position between two somewhat untrustworthy elements, was looking to her armaments. The Polish forces owned a heterogeneous collection of almost every pistol on earth, and in the early 1930s a competition was announced for a new standard service pistol. Various companies put forward designs, but the winners were two Poles, Wilniewczyc and Skrzpinski, who submitted a 9-mm pistol based somewhat on Browning's 1927 patent. The barrel locked to the slide by ribs and was withdrawn by the same shaped cam as used in the GP Model 35. Other refinements included a hammer release catch which could be pressed, after the safety was applied, to lower the hammer on to a loaded chamber so that it could be readily cocked when needed. This pistol went into production as the VIS-35, and some 33,500 had been made and issued by the outbreak of war in 1939.

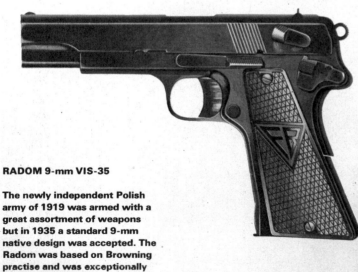

RADOM 9-mm VIS-35

The newly independent Polish army of 1919 was armed with a great assortment of weapons but in 1935 a standard 9-mm native design was accepted. The Radom was based on Browning practise and was exceptionally strong and reliable

Weight: 2 lb 5 oz
Muzzle velocity: 850 fps
Magazine: 8 shots

TOKAREV 7.62-mm MODEL TT33

The Tokarev was the Soviet Army's standard pistol from 1933 until the 1950s. Basically it uses the Colt 'swinging link' system of locking the barrel to the slide, but has a few innovations of its own. The most original feature is the assembly of the lockwork and hammer into a complete removable module which can be slipped out of the frame for cleaning or repair very easily. The whole design has been arranged for easy mass production; one example – the locking ribs on the barrel go all round, so that they can be cut on a lathe, instead of, as in the Colt, being milled on top of the barrel only. A Hungarian firm made an interesting variant of this in 9-mm calibre for the Egyptian Army in the 1950s, called the Tokagypt

Weight: 1 lb 13 oz

Muzzle velocity: 1375 fps

Magazine: 8 shots

BERETTA

The Beretta Model 34 pistol became the standard Italian Army pistol in 1934. Chambered for the 9-mm Short cartridge, it became the pattern for several subsequent Beretta models

Weight: 1 lb 7½ oz

Muzzle velocity: 825 fps

Magazine: 7 shots

One more 1935 design deserves mention, the Finnish Lahti M-35. The Finns had used the 7.65-mm Parabellum for many years, but its toggle-lock was not the best mechanism in sub-zero weather and arctic blizzards, and they sought a replacement. Aimo Lahti, a noted Finn arms designer, began work in 1929 and the pistol was eventually put into production in 1935. In outline it resembles the Parabellum, but the mechanism is much different, more akin to an early Bergmann. The square-section receiver conceals a bolt which is locked by a U-shaped yoke, and the action is unusual in having a bolt accelerator. This is a cam-shaped arm which is struck by the recoiling barrel and develops a gain in leverage which thrusts the bolt back much more quickly than could be achieved by simple recoil. It also gives the bolt a useful reserve of power to overcome any stickiness caused by extreme cold. The action is well sealed up against dirt and wet; the only drawback seems to be that it is almost impossible to dismantle without access to a workshop and some tools, but it is so reliable that it rarely needs dismantling.

The civil market for pistols was given a shock in 1929 when the German firm of Carl Walther unveiled their latest design. Walther had been producing very simple, though well-made and reliable, blowback pocket pistols since 1908, but they now introduced a most sophisticated design, the Model PP or Polizei Pistole, in 7.65-mm calibre. The outstanding feature of this weapon, besides its generally streamlined and modern appearance, was that it incorporated a double-action lock. Except for a few experimental designs and one (the Little Tom) which had achieved some reasonable sales every automatic

pistol so far available had needed two hands to get it into action. You grasped the butt and pulled back the slide with the other hand to charge a cartridge into the action and cock the hammer. Having done that you applied the safety catch and put the pistol back into the holster, or you began firing. Either way, it had its drawbacks. If you needed to go into action quickly against an opponent, time was wasted while the pistol was cocked, time in which you were likely to lose interest in the results. If the pistol was not needed immediately there were drawbacks in carrying it around with the action cocked, even with safety catch applied.

Walther's design changed all this. The magazine was placed in the butt and the slide pulled back and released in the usual way, putting a cartridge in the chamber; this you did well before the need arose for firing it. The safety catch, which, unusually, was on the slide and not on the frame, was then pressed down; this first locked the firing pin securely; then it rotated a steel block behind the firing pin; and then it tripped the hammer so that it fell on to the steel block. The pistol could then be holstered and carried. There was a round in the chamber, but the hammer was down, resting on a steel block; the trigger was locked; and the hammer was locked. It couldn't be safer. When action called, the pistol was drawn, the safety catch pushed off, and the trigger pulled; this first lifted the hammer to full cock and then dropped it to fire the chambered cartridge. After that the slide recoiled and cocked the hammer for each shot in the normal way. Another advantage was that if the cartridge happened to misfire, a smart pull of the trigger gave the cap another bang, and this very

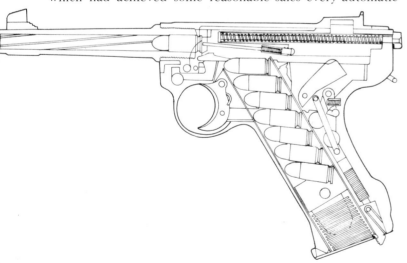

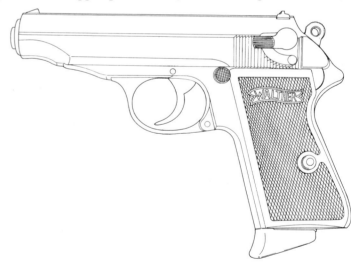

LAHTI 9-mm MODEL 35

The Lahti comes from Finland and is among the top-quality military pistols of the world. It uses a recoiling bolt and sliding yoke to lock it, and is unusual in having a bolt accelerator to ensure positive action in sub-zero weather. It was adopted by the Finns in 1935; the Swedes decided to adopt it in 1940, but since the Finns could not produce them, they obtained a licence to

manufacture in Sweden. Unfortunately they could not obtain the special Finnish steels, nor the special Finnish know-how, and the Swedish Model 40 was never as good as the genuine model

Weight: 2 lb 11 oz

Muzzle velocity: 1150 fps

Magazine: 8 shots

WALTHER 7.65-mm MODEL PP

Walther's Polizei Pistole of 1929 broke new ground by introducing a practical double-action lock and giving the weapon an attractive 'streamlined' appearance. Widely adopted by police forces as a holster pistol, it also sold well on the commercial market. Models in 6.35-mm, 9-mm Short and .22 Long Rifle calibre were also made, though in lesser quantities

Weight: 1 lb 9 oz

Muzzle velocity: 950 fps

Magazine: 8 shots

often was enough to make it fire. This could be a very useful feature in both police work and combat equally.

The Walther PP was an immediate success and was widely adopted by police forces all over Europe. It was followed rapidly by a smaller edition, the Model PPK or Pistole Polizei Kriminal, signifying that it was intended for use by plain-clothes police officers. This was also in 7.65-mm calibre and used the same double-action lock; in fact the only significant change was in the method of building the frame; in the PP the butt was a continuous steel outline with plastic buttplates screwed to each side. This design was followed in the first PPKs but it was soon changed to a design in which there was no backstrap to the butt and the plastic grip was a one-piece wrap-around unit which gave a very comfortable grip.

Less well known but equally efficient was the Sauer Model 38, which, as the title implies, appeared almost ten years after the Walther design. The Sauer company had also been in the pocket pistol business since before the First World War and for much of the time their 7.65-mm Behorden Modell had been the preferred police weapon. With their sales rapidly dwindling in favour of Walther, they now designed a completely new pistol which achieved much the same results as the PP but in a different manner – mainly because Walther had, of course, secured patents on his design. The Sauer 38 was another modern-looking weapon, half an inch longer than the Walther but almost the same weight. It had a similar slide-mounted safety catch, but the hammer was concealed inside the frame and there was a peculiar thumb-lever under the left grip and protruding just behind the trigger in a posi-

tion in which the right thumb fell on to it naturally when the pistol was gripped for firing.

The Sauer was loaded in the usual way – magazine in the butt and the slide pulled back and released. Now, if the trigger was pulled back slightly so as to take up the slack against the cocked hammer, and the thumb lever firmly held, the trigger could then be pulled to release the hammer but it was blocked from falling by the thumb lever; and by easing the lever up under the thumb, so the hammer could be lowered safely on to the firing pin. Safely, because the firing pin was shorter than the distance from the face of the hammer to the cartridge cap; therefore when the hammer rested on the pin, the tip did not protrude to strike the cap. Only when the hammer fell with force to hit the pin did it drive it far enough forward to contact the cap and fire it. The safety catch could now be applied to lock everything solid. When required to fire, the user had two options. If he was in a hurry, he simply pulled the trigger and the double-action lock raised the hammer and released it to fire the pistol; if he wanted to take a more deliberate aim, he could press down on the thumb lever which lifted the hammer to full-cock, then take aim and press the trigger. Altogether the Sauer was a first-class design which would have given the Walther PP a good run for its money but for one thing; it appeared just before the outbreak of war, and before it had time to make any impression on the civil market, its entire output was taken by the German forces.

By 1938 the German forces were taking every pistol they could get their hands on. Until 1933 the service weapon had been the Pistole '08 and nobody ever thought otherwise, but

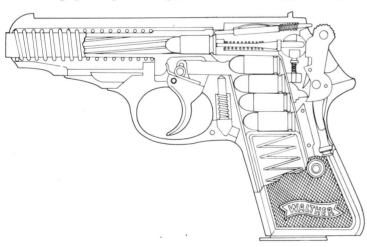

WALTHER 7.65-mm MODEL PPK

After the success of the PP Model for uniformed police, Walther followed it with this smaller version for plain-clothes-men *(Pistole Polizei Kriminale, CID)*. It was available in the same calibres and, like the PP was continued after a short post-war break. In the USA this pistol is too small to be imported and a special version, the PPK/S, is made up from the frame of the

PP and the slide of the PPK in order to qualify for importation under the Gun Control Act of 1968

Weight: 1 lb 5 oz

Muzzle velocity: 950 fps

Magazine: 7 shots

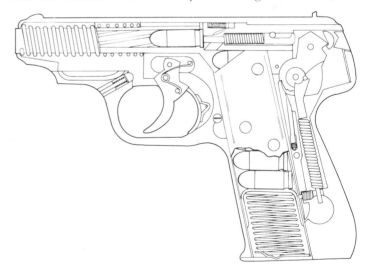

SAUER & SOHN 7.65-mm MODEL 38H

Sauer & Sohn are an old-established German gunmaking firm, and this automatic pistol appeared in 1938, to compete with the Walther PP. It used a double-action lock with a concealed hammer which could be locked or released under control by a thumb-lever under the left grip. Although sold commercially, most of the

production was taken by the German Armed Forces

Weight: 1 lb 10 oz

Muzzle velocity: 900 fps

Magazine: 7 shots

An American MP brings in
German prisoners from a
French farmhouse – at the
point of a captured P-38

Keystone

when the expansion of the German army began it became obvious that the production of P'08s could not keep pace. The Parabellum had not been designed with an eye to mass-production, and the Wehrmacht wanted something easier, cheaper and quicker to make.

Walther had foreseen this and they were already working on potential designs. Their first attempt was simply to beef up the PP and build it in 9-mm Parabellum calibre, but although it worked, there was no chance of the Army's accepting an unlocked blowback pistol with a cartridge of that power; they had tried that in the last war and it wasn't a good idea. So Walther had to set about designing a locked-breech pistol for the first time, and managed to produce something totally new, which they called the Model AP for Armee Pistole. The AP consisted of three basic groups; the frame, the slide, and the barrel. The rear end of the barrel was shaped into bearing surfaces which rode in grooves in the front section of the slide. The slide acted as the breechblock in its rear section and had most of the forward portion cut away at the top so as to allow ejection of spent cases, and the whole slide ran back and forth on top of the frame. Beneath the barrel was a wedge-shaped locking unit which was driven up and down by shaped surfaces in the forward end of the frame; with the slide forward and the breech closed, this wedge was forced up so that vertical portions entered into slots in the side of the slide. Since the wedge was hinged to the barrel, the slide and barrel were thus locked firmly together. On firing, the barrel and slide would recoil for a short distance, after which the wedge would drop and release the slide; the dropped wedge came up against a spring buffer in the frame which stopped the barrel moving, while the slide went back, cocking the hammer, and then returned, driven by two recoil springs, to load a fresh

WALTHER 9-mm MODEL P-38

The P-38 was adopted by the German Army as a replacement for the Parabellum P-08 since it was cheaper and easier to mass-produce. It uses the double-action lock which Walther pioneered in their Model PP and acquired a good reputation for reliability and accuracy. Since the war it has been re-adopted by the Bundeswehr as their P-1 pistol, and in the past it was used by

Sweden and several other countries. It is now made in .22 and 7.65-mm Parabellum calibres, and a recent addition is the P38K, a short-barrelled version in 9 mm

Weight: 2 lb 2 oz	
Muzzle velocity: 1150 fps	
Magazine: 8 shots	

German SS panzer-grenadiers pictured during the Ardennes offensive of 1944 armed with a Browning Hi-Power, manufactured by FN in occupied Liège for the German army

Imperial War Museum

cartridge into the chamber and then close and lock the breech. The lock, needless to say, was the same double-action device as used on the PP, though in this design the hammer was concealed under the slide.

The Army liked it but for the concealed hammer; this feature was objected to on two grounds, firstly that you couldn't see whether the pistol was cocked or not, and secondly that it was not possible to cock the hammer for a deliberate shot. So Walther took the pistol back and redesigned it with an external hammer, calling this the Model HP for Heeres Pistole. This was approved, and the HP became the Pistole 38 or P-38. Production began in the summer of 1939, though it was not formally introduced for service until April 1940. Strangely, for all the Army's desperate needs, Walther were permitted to sell the pistol commercially; it was advertised in New York (for $75) and some were supplied to the Swedish Army in 1939. But from 1940 onwards, all supplies went to the armed forces of Germany. It has been estimated that 1.24 million were made by 1945, but even this could not keep pace with demand and although it was supposed to have replaced the Pistole '08, in fact the Parabellum stayed in production until the end of 1944. And when the postwar German Army was reconstituted in the 1950s, the pistol they demanded was the P-38, now known as the P-1 and very slightly modified, still made by the same firm.

The Second World War saw little in the way of pistol development, but, just as the First World War, it made demands on production that had to be met by inducting all sorts of pistols. The German Army overran Poland and Belgium and were only too happy to keep the local factories at work producing Browning GP 35 and VIS 35 pistols, stamped with German Army markings and taken straight into German Army use. The British Army had abandoned the .455 Webley in the 1930s, since they considered that it was too much gun for hastily-trained wartime troops and that a .38 firing a heavy lead bullet could probably stop men just as easily. The .38 revolver they adopted was basically a Webley but with the lockwork redesigned by the Royal Small Arms Factory at Enfield, so it became known as the Enfield. But in the rush of war, these were not sufficient and the Webley factory were called on to produce their own .38 revolver for the Army. In addition, purchasing missions roved far and wide and bought pistols where they could; one oddity was the Argentinian Ballester-Molina, a local copy of the Colt M1911 in .45 calibre, several hundred of which appeared in Britain. Another, of less dubious ancestry, was the .38 Smith & Wesson 38/200, a variant of their standard Military and Police chambered to take the British 200-grain .38 cartridge; 1,125,000 of these were bought, and proved very popular with the British troops who used them.

One strange field of endeavour was the supplying of pistols to Continental resistance groups and partisans of one sort and another. Civilian weapons were bought for this purpose, but the Americans decided to produce a simple mass-produced pistol for the task and set about designing the Flare Projector or Liberator M1942 pistol. This was stamped out by the million and consisted of nothing more than a pistol-shaped steel pressing containing a smooth bore barrel, a hand-cocked firing pin, and a compartment in the butt to carry a few loose cartridges. It was in .45 automatic pistol chambering, and to use it you merely pulled back the breech, inserted

WEBLEY .38 MK 4

After the First World War the British Army decided to change to .38 calibre, and Webley designed this revolver. It was not accepted for military use and went on the market for sale to police forces and private shooters. But during the Second World War, faced with a shortage of revolvers, the British Army changed their mind and the Webley was officially adopted

Weight: 1 lb 11 oz

Muzzle velocity: 600 fps

Cylinder: 6 shots

SMITH & WESSON .38

Smith & Wesson received large orders from embattled Britain in 1940 and they supplied their standard model chambered for the British .38 cartridge. The weapon was highly popular and much preferred to the Enfield

Weight: 1 lb 8 oz	
Muzzle velocity: 1125 fps	
Magazine: 6 shots	

ENFIELD .38 PISTOL, REVOLVER, NO 2 MK 1

Instead of taking the Webley design in the 1920s, the British Army decided to try for an 'in-house' design instead and asked the Royal Small Arms Factory at Enfield Lock to produce a revolver. The result looked much the same as the Webley but had a few small changes in the trigger mechanism. Introduced in 1932, a later variation was the Mark 1* in which the hammer spur was removed, so that Royal Tank Corps crews were less likely to snag the hammer on the tank's internal fittings

Weight: 1 lb 11 oz	
Muzzle velocity: 650 fps	
Cylinder: 6 shots	

a cartridge into the chamber, closed the breech and pulled the trigger. Having fired, the breech was opened and a convenient stick or pencil was used to poke down the barrel and eject the spent case. It was provided with a comic-strip set of instructions which could be understood by a complete illiterate, and these pistols were distributed around the world by the carload. Provided you got within six feet of your target and did not miss, they were effective; but if you missed with the first shot, there was small chance of getting through the eject and reload routine to get off a second shot.

The Germans, toward the end of the war, began looking at pistol designs that could be stamped out quickly by factories without much knowledge of the pistol business. Walther developed a pressed-steel version of the PP chambered for 9-mm Parabellum, but the Army turned it down. Mauser then produced their Volkspistole, also made largely from stamped-metal components but using an ingenious delayed blowback system. It fired the standard 9-mm cartridge and the slide fitted quite tightly around the fixed barrel except for an enlarged area just in front of the breech. Here there were gas

escape holes and when the pistol fired, some of the gas passed through these holes and into the space between the slide and the barrel, there building up pressure against the front end of the slide which resisted the opening action until the chamber pressure had dropped. It was an ingenious idea, but before the wrinkles could be got out of it the war had ended.

When the Germans moved into Belgium, some of the engineers from Fabrique National escaped to Britain with GP-35 pistols and drawings. For a short time there was debate about whether it might not be put into production in Britain, but facilities were not available and the design was sent to Canada, where the John Inglis Company, of Toronto, put it into production, firstly for the Chinese Nationalist Army who had adopted the weapon in 1938 and were anxious to obtain more supplies. Once this demand had been met, Inglis continued producing them, supplies going to the Canadian Army and then to the British Army for use by Airborne and other special forces. This adoption seems to have been the proving ground for the automatic pistol in British service, and ten years later the GP-35 became the standard British pistol.

The military revolver with its advantages of reliability and durability proved itself in two world wars – in the mud of the trenches and the dust and sand of the desert. This British officer in the Western Desert, 1942 is armed with a Webley, standard equipment since 1880

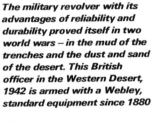

THE OSS FLARE PROJECTOR OR LIBERATOR

This single-shot terrorist weapon was developed secretly during the war under the title of Flare Projector and was for dropping into enemy-occupied territory to provide the local resistance with a simple means of retaliation. It was loaded one shot at a time and the empty case had to be poked out of the barrel with a stick. At a price of $2.10 it was not the cheapest pistol in history but it must be one of the most widely distributed

Weight: 1 lb	
Muzzle velocity: 820 fps	
Magazine: none	

NEW TECHNOLOGY, NEW TARGET

One of the first postwar pistols to appear was a Swiss design, the SIG (Schweizerische Industrie-Gesellschaft), which had a curious history dating back to the early 1930s. The French Army had begun looking for an automatic pistol at this time and in 1934 a design was patented by Charles Petter, an enigmatic Swiss who came into gun designing by way of the French Foreign Legion, among other activities. He was an employee of the Société Alsacienne de Construction Mécanique (SACM) and his design, like so many others of the period, leaned heavily on Browning's 1927 patent in so far as it used a fixed cam beneath the breech to withdraw the barrel and unlock it. The design was adopted by the French Army as their Modèle 1935 and production got under way, more than 40,000 being made before the German occupation. Since the rate of production did not look like being enough, the design was simplified by the Government arsenal of St. Etienne, this version being the M1935S, while the original became the M1935A. Except for the fact that it was chambered for a peculiar French cartridge, the 7.65-mm Longue, it was a sound design.

During the war the Swiss realised that there were designs of pistol appearing which made their 7.65-mm Parabellum service pistol look dated, and the Swiss Army began tests to select a new design. To compete, the SIG company looked at what was available and decided that the Petter design was worth following up; they therefore negotiated with the French in 1940 and bought the rights to the Petter patents. Development followed, and in 1944 some Neuhausen 44/16 pistols were tested; the name came from the location of the SIG factory and the fact that the magazines held 16 rounds. These were followed by the Neuhausen 44/8 model, and the Swiss Army conducted trials. No conclusive result appeared, so SIG made more modifications to the design and in 1948 placed the result on the market as the SIG SP 47/8 in 9-mm Parabellum calibre, with the option of changing to 7.65-mm Parabellum calibre by simply changing the barrel and recoil spring.

The SP 47/8 was based on the Browning dropping barrel with cam, as were the original Petter and the GP-35, and had the hammer, sear, and other lock components in a removable action casing. The most unusual feature of the design was that the slide ran on rails formed on the inside of the frame instead of the more usual method of having the slide sides overlap the frame and ride on the outside. Though this system is more difficult and expensive to manufacture, it gives better support to the recoiling parts and it materially aids in the SIG's reputation for longevity and high accuracy.

The SP47/8 was adopted by the Swiss Army in 1948; soon afterwards it was adopted by the West German Border Police and by the Danish Army. Apart from these it has rarely been adopted for military or police purposes, principally because it is too good and too expensive. But it was rapidly taken to by target shooters and those who appreciated fine workmanship. At present the SIG P-210 (its present title) retails in the USA for $650 in its cheapest form, a sum which would buy three or four of its nearest rivals, but for all that it seems to sell. If you build a better mousetrap . . .

The war exposed a lot of people to firearms who otherwise might never have given them a thought, and, as a result, there has been no shortage of new ideas in the ensuing years. In the pistol field there are two new approaches which deserve mention, even though neither of them had the success hoped

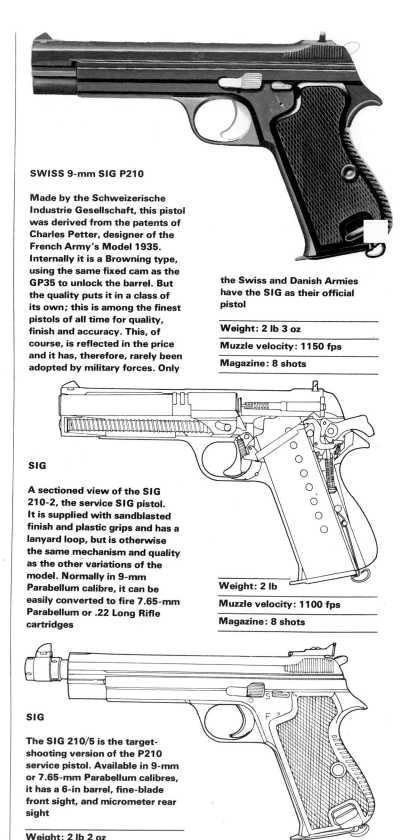

SWISS 9-mm SIG P210

Made by the Schweizerische Industrie Gesellschaft, this pistol was derived from the patents of Charles Petter, designer of the French Army's Model 1935. Internally it is a Browning type, using the same fixed cam as the GP35 to unlock the barrel. But the quality puts it in a class of its own; this is among the finest pistols of all time for quality, finish and accuracy. This, of course, is reflected in the price and it has, therefore, rarely been adopted by military forces. Only the Swiss and Danish Armies have the SIG as their official pistol

Weight: 2 lb 3 oz

Muzzle velocity: 1150 fps

Magazine: 8 shots

SIG

A sectioned view of the SIG 210-2, the service SIG pistol. It is supplied with sandblasted finish and plastic grips and has a lanyard loop, but is otherwise the same mechanism and quality as the other variations of the model. Normally in 9-mm Parabellum calibre, it can be easily converted to fire 7.65-mm Parabellum or .22 Long Rifle cartridges

Weight: 2 lb

Muzzle velocity: 1100 fps

Magazine: 8 shots

SIG

The SIG 210/5 is the target-shooting version of the P210 service pistol. Available in 9-mm or 7.65-mm Parabellum calibres, it has a 6-in barrel, fine-blade front sight, and micrometer rear sight

Weight: 2 lb 2 oz

Muzzle velocity: 1135 fps

Magazine: 8 shots

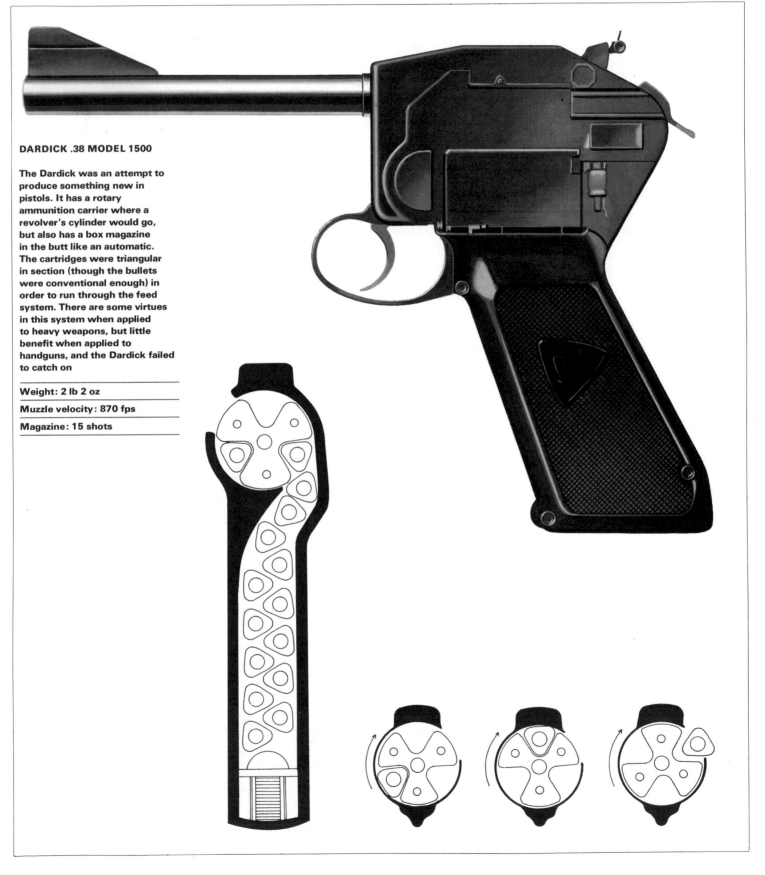

DARDICK .38 MODEL 1500

The Dardick was an attempt to produce something new in pistols. It has a rotary ammunition carrier where a revolver's cylinder would go, but also has a box magazine in the butt like an automatic. The cartridges were triangular in section (though the bullets were conventional enough) in order to run through the feed system. There are some virtues in this system when applied to heavy weapons, but little benefit when applied to handguns, and the Dardick failed to catch on

Weight: 2 lb 2 oz

Muzzle velocity: 870 fps

Magazine: 15 shots

for by their inventors. The Dardick pistol appeared in the US in the 1950s and introduced a new mechanical principle, that of the open-chamber gun. Basically it was a revolver, in so far as it had a fixed barrel with a revolving unit behind it and a hammer behind that. But the magazine was a box that went into the butt in the same manner as an automatic pistol, and the revolving section was a feed system and chamber. This revolving section had but three chambers, which were not the usual longitudinal holes but were triangular-shaped recesses in the revolving block. As the cartridges fed up from the magazine, the topmost cartridge entered the recess above it. Pulling the trigger moved the revolving unit round to present this cartridge behind the barrel and drop the hammer to fire it. The top strap of the pistol acted as the third side of the triangular recess, making it into the firing chamber. While the shot took place, the next round had entered the next recess. The next pull of the trigger brought the second round up to be fired, and moving the first recess past an aperture, allowed the empty case of the first shot to be ejected.

The important feature of the Dardick gun was that the cartridges had to be triangular in section to fit snugly into the recesses in the feed revolver, and this was done by inserting standard cartridges into polycarbonate sleeves of the right shape. These also strengthened the case against the explosion so that the open chamber concept was safe. Moreover it meant that many of the components could be of a standard size, since cartridges of various calibres could be fitted into one size of 'tround', as the triangular sleeves were called. The Dardick pistol was produced in .38 calibre as standard, adapters and spare barrels being available to convert to 9-mm or .22 chambering. But it was a little too unusual for most people, and it was also expensive, and after about five years the pistol went off the market.

Even more exotic was the Gyrojet pistol developed by MBA Associates, of California. It looked like a pistol and the ammunition was loaded into the butt, but that was about as far as the term pistol is relevant. It was, in fact, a hand-held rocket launcher. The rockets were 13-mm in diameter and had a solid head and tubular body in which was a solid charge of propellant. The base was closed by a venturi plate with four angled vents and a central percussion cap. The whole rocket was about an inch and a half long. When the trigger was pulled a hammer came up and hit the chambered rocket on the nose, driving it back so that the cap struck a fixed firing pin. This ignited the rocket motor, the blast exited via the angled vents, and the rocket took off down the 'barrel' of the 'pistol', pushing down the hammer and thus recocking it as it went. The angled vents caused it to spin as well as travel forward and the rocket reached maximum velocity some distance from the launcher.

The Gyrojet pistol was put on the market in 1965 and at first it sold well on its novelty value. But hopes of military adoption were dashed by the poor accuracy and the fall-off in velocity once the rocket was burned out, and, again, after about five years the project foundered.

One idea which has popped up at various times has been the possibility of turning an automatic pistol into a sub-machine-gun. As we have seen, the 'automatic', as we call it, isn't really automatic at all; it is, strictly, a self-loader and it gets that way because the designer carefully fits in a component called a disconnector to make sure that the firer

SOVIET 9-mm STETCHKIN

Sooner or later most people are tempted to turn a decent pistol into a second-rate submachine-gun, and this is the Soviet entry in this field. Basically it was derived from the Walther PP design but rather larger and without the double-action lock. Instead the safety catch has three positions, the extra one giving full-automatic fire. A wooden holster-stock like that of the Mauser Military pistol was supplied, and with it fitted, the Stetchkin could be fired at 725 rpm with some sort of control. Without the butt, however, it was completely uncontrollable. Recent information indicates that, having satisfied the urge, the Soviets are now getting rid of it

Weight: 1 lb 10 oz

Muzzle velocity: 1115 fps

Magazine: 20 shots

SOVIET 9-mm MAKAROV

The Soviet Makarov resembles the Walther PP design in many ways, though some of the internal firing mechanism linkage is different. The same double-action lock is employed, though the Makarov safety moves in the opposite direction to that of the Walther. The most interesting feature of this pistol when it was introduced was the new cartridge, 9-mm x 18-mm case length; this is half way between the 9-mm Short and the 9-mm Parabellum and was probably chosen as being the most powerful cartridge capable of being fired from a relatively simple blowback pistol

Weight: 1 lb 9 oz

Muzzle velocity: 1075 fps

Magazine: 8 shots

GYROJET 13-mm MARK 1 HANDGUN

Another attempt to introduce something new into the handgun world was this hand-held rocket launcher. The spin-stabilised rocket was slightly bigger than a conventional .45 cartridge. As well as being made in handgun form, it could also be turned into a carbine, but the idea failed to attract many customers due to lack of accuracy

Weight: 1 lb

Muzzle velocity: 1250 fps

Magazine: 5 shots

HECKLER & KOCH 9-mm MODEL P9S

This is a locked-breech model, using the same system of roller locking that Heckler & Koch use on their G3 rifle. It fires by a concealed hammer, and the thumb lever on the left grip allows the hammer to be cocked or uncocked at will. The lock is double-action, so that the shooter has a variety of options for firing the pistol. A P9 model is available in single-action-only form. The pistol is currently in use by the German Border Police and other police forces. It has also been produced in .45 calibre, particularly for sale in the USA

Weight: 2 lb

Muzzle velocity: 1150 fps

Magazine: 9 shots

has to release the trigger after each shot before he can fire another. But if you take out the disconnector, then one squeeze of the trigger and the pistol will continue to fire until the magazine is empty or until the pressure on the trigger is released; and generally speaking, the magazine empties first. This is simply because of the lightweight breech of a pistol, compared with the working parts of, say, a machine-gun. The lightweight breech runs back and forth so fast, and a pistol magazine holds so few rounds, that the magazine is empty in about half a second. The first attempts to make fully-automatic pistols were during the First World War when it was thought that they might make useful weapons for fliers, but that idea soon died. They reappeared in Spain in the late 1920s with a rash of cheap copies of the Mauser C/96 Military with removable magazines holding 20 or 30 rounds and selector switches which allowed single shots or automatic fire. These became so common that Mauser, in self defence, had to produce one to keep their markets. With a sizable magazine and the wooden butt-stock fitted, they were just about practical, but apart from some sold to Nicaragua and Jugoslavia, they saw little serious use.

In postwar years the idea appeared again, this time in Russia, when the Soviet Army adopted the Stetchkin pistol. This resembled an overgrown Walther PP but fired a special 9-mm cartridge of Soviet origin, shorter than the 9-mm Parabellum but more powerful than the 9-mm Short. Fitted with a wooden butt, the Stechkin doubled as a submachine-gun, but it seems not to have found favour and went out of service as abruptly as it came in.

A possible solution to the problem has recently appeared in Germany, the Heckler & Koch VP-70 pistol. This uses an 18-shot magazine and is chambered for the 9-mm Parabellum cartridge. It can be used as a normal automatic pistol, having a rather unusual double-action-only lock in which the first pressure of the trigger cocks a striker and further pressure then releases it to fire the round. But an accessory plastic butt can be fitted to the rear of the pistol, and when this is done, a special connection is made with the lock-work which brings into play a burst-fire device. With this engaged, every pressure on the trigger fires three shots in a rapid burst. Thus there is the rapid delivery of multiple shots which, it is hoped, will hit the target, but the waste of ammunition and the uncontrollable jump of the average converted pistol is absent, so that there is the chance to re-aim and fire another burst with minimum delay. At present the VP-70 is being evaluated by various military agencies.

The revolver, of course, continues on its way without having altered much since the turn of the century; the only major changes have been in methods of manufacture, not in methods of operation, since making revolvers in the traditional way is an expensive matter. Such things as precision casting and alloys are coming into prominence in this field.

While the use of handguns in military circles is declining in favour of submachine-guns and assault rifles, the sport use of handguns, for target shooting and hunting, is growing daily. New designs of automatic pistols appear almost every month, new revolvers almost as rapidly, most of them being intended for either sport or police use. In spite of legislation, the handgun appears to be in a healthy condition, and it will be interesting to see if the next hundred years will prove as technically interesting as have the last.

Camera Press

Big city, USA, and a Private Investigator cruising the neon-lit streets, carries a Colt Detective Special, with its short snout designed to slip easily into a 'speed' – holster

SMITH & WESSON .44 MAGNUM MODEL 29

This is one of the world's most powerful handguns, and probably one of the best-made and most beautifully finished pistols available today. The .44 Magnum cartridge was developed by Remington in 1955 and the Model 29 was produced in order to fire it. It is a heavy gun, as it needs to be to soak up some of the recoil, and firing it has been compared to touching off a howitzer one-handed. For those requiring something less devastating, the .44 Special or .44 Russian cartridges can be fired in this pistol, delivering rather less recoil

Weight:	2 lb 14 oz
Muzzle velocity:	1540 fps
Cylinder:	6 shots

COLT .38 DETECTIVE SPECIAL

Colt's Detective Special was first introduced in 1927, when plain-clothes detectives were demanding short-barrelled pistols they could conceal easily. It was little more than the contemporary Police Positive Special with the barrel length reduced to two inches. The advantage lay in the fact that although a small weapon in length, it still had full-sized grips to give a firm hold for quick shooting. It has been periodically updated and the current model is chambered for the .38 Special cartridge, though a .32 is also available

Weight:	1 lb 5 oz
Muzzle velocity:	870 fps
Cylinder:	6 shots

127

Artwork Index